Sejanus
His Fall

By
Ben Jonson

ANODOS BOOKS
Candida Casa

Ben Jonson (1572-1637)
Originally published in 1605
Editing, cover, and internal design by Alisdair MacNoravaich for Anodos Books.
Copyright © 2017 Anodos Books. All rights reserved.

Anodos Books
1c Kings Road
Whithorn
Newton Stewart
Dumfries & Galloway
DG8 8PP

Contents

TO THE READERS	1
THE ARGUMENT	3
DRAMATIS PERSONAE	5
ACT I	6
ACT II	27
ACT III	45
ACT IV	69
ACT V	87

TO THE READERS

THE following and voluntary labours of my friends, prefixed to my book, have relieved me in much whereat, without them, I should necessarily have touched. Now I will only use three or four short and needful notes, and so rest.

First, if it be objected, that what I publish is no true poem, in the strict laws of time, I confess it: as also in the want of a proper chorus; whose habit and moods are such and so difficult, as not any, whom I have seen, since the ancients, no, not they who have most presently affected laws, have yet come in the way of. Nor is it needful, or almost possible in these our times, and to such auditors as commonly things are presented, to observe the old state and splendour of dramatic poems, with preservation of any popular delight. But of this I shall take more seasonable cause to speak, in my observations upon Horace his Art of Poetry, which, with the text translated, I intend shortly to publish. In the mean time, if in truth of argument, dignity of persons, gravity and height of elocution, fulness and frequency of sentence, I have discharged the other offices of a tragic writer, let not the absence of these forms be imputed to me, wherein I shall give you occasion hereafter, and without my boast, to think I could better prescribe, than omit the due use for want of a convenient knowledge.

The next is, lest in some nice nostril the quotations might savour affected, I do let you know, that I abhor nothing more; and I have only done it to shew my integrity in the story, and save myself in those common torturers that bring all wit to the rack; whose noses are ever like swine, spoiling and rooting up the Muses' gardens; and their whole bodies like moles, as blindly working under earth, to cast any, the least, hills upon virtue. Whereas they are in Latin, and the work in English, it was presupposed none but the learned would take the pains to confer them: the authors themselves being all in the learned tongues, save one, with whose English side I have had little to do. To which it may be required, since I have quoted the page, to name what editions I followed: Tacit. Lips. in quarto, Antwerp, edit. 1600; Dio. folio, Hen. Steph. 1592. For the rest, as Sueton, Seneca, etc., the chapter doth sufficiently direct, or the edition is not varied.

Lastly, I would inform you, that this book, in all numbers, is not the same with that which was acted on the public stage; wherein a second: pen had good share: in place of which, I have rather chosen to put weaker, and no doubt, less pleasing, of mine own, than to defraud so happy a genius of his right by my loathed usurpation.

Fare you well, and if you read farther of me, and like, I shall not be afraid of it, though you praise me out.

Neque enim mihi cornea fibra est.

But that I should plant my felicity in your general saying, good, or well, etc., were a weakness which the better sort of you might worthily contemn, if not absolutely hate me for.

BEN JONSON;

and no such,

Quem
Palma negata macrum, donata reducit opimum.

THE ARGUMENT

AELIUS SEJANUS, son to Seius Strabo, a gentleman of Rome, and born at Vulsinium; after his long service in court, first under Augustus; afterward, Tiberius; grew into that favour with the latter, and won him by those arts, as there wanted nothing but the name to make him a co-partner of the empire. Which greatness of his, Drusus, the emperor's son, not brooking; after many smothered dislikes, it one day breaking out, the prince struck him publicly on the face. To revenge which disgrace, Livia, the wife of Drusus (being before corrupted by him to her dishonour, and the discovery of her husband's counsels) Sejanus practiseth with, together with her physician called Eudemus, and one Lygdus an eunuch, to poison Drusus. This their inhuman act having successful and unsuspected passage, it emboldeneth Sejanus to further and more insolent projects, even the ambition of the empire; where finding the lets he must encounter to be many and hard, in respect of the issue of Germanicus, who were next in hope for the succession, he deviseth to make Tiberius' self his means, and instils into his ears many doubts and suspicions, both against the princes, and their mother Agrippina; which Caesar jealously hearkening to, as covetously consenteth to their ruin, and their friends. In this time, the better to mature and strengthen his design, Sejanus labours to marry Livia, and worketh with all his ingine, to remove Tiberius from the knowledge of public business, with allurements of a quiet and retired life; the latter of which, Tiberius, out of a proneness to lust, and a desire to hide those unnatural pleasures which he could not so publicly practise, embraceth: the former enkindleth his fears, and there gives him first cause of doubt or suspect towards Sejanus: against whom he raiseth in private a new instrument, one Sertorius Macro, and by him underworketh, discovers the other's counsels, his means, his ends, sounds the affections of the senators, divides, distracts them: at last, when Sejanus least looketh, and is most secure with pretext of doing him an unwonted honour in the senate, he trains him from his guards, and with a long doubtful letter, one day hath him suspected, accused, condemned, and torn in pieces by the rage of the people.

DRAMATIS PERSONAE

TIBERIUS.
DRUSUS SENIOR.
NERO.
DRUSUS JUNIOR.
CALIGULA.
LUCIUS ARRUNTIUS.
CAIUS SILIUS.
TITIUS SABINUS.
MARCUS LEPIDUS.
CREMUTIUS CORDUS.
ASINIUS GALLUS.
REGULUS.
TERENTIUS.
GRACINUS LACO.
EUDEMUS.
RUFUS.
SEJANUS.
LATIARIS.
VARRO.
SERTORIUS MACRO.
COTTA.
DOMITIUS AFER.

HATERIUS.
SANQUINIUS.
POMPONIUS.
JULIUS POSTHUMUS.
FULCINIUS TRIO.
MINUTIUS.
SATRIUS SECUNDUS.
PINNARIUS NATTA.
OPSIUS.
Tribuni.
Praecones.
Flamen.
Tubicines.
Nuntius.
Lictores.
Minisri.
Tibicines.
Servi etc.

AGRIPPINA.
LIVIA.
SOSIA.

SCENE,-ROME

ACT I

SCENE I.-A State Room in the Palace.
Enter SABINUS and SILIUS, followed by LATIARIS.

Sab. Hail, Caius Silius!

Sil. Titius Sabinus, hail! You're rarely met in court.

Sab. Therefore, well met.

Sil. 'Tis true: indeed, this place is not our sphere.

Sab.
　No, Silius, we are no good inginers.
　We want their fine arts, and their thriving use
　Should make us graced, or favour'd of the times:
　We have no shift of faces, no cleft tongues,
　No soft and glutinous bodies, that can stick,
　Like snails on painted walls; or, on our breasts,
　Creep up, to fall from that proud height, to which
　We did by slavery, not by service climb.
　We are no guilty men, and then no great;
　We have no place in court, office In state,
　That we can say, we owe unto our crimes:
　We burn with no black secrets, which can make
　Us dear to the pale authors; or live fear'd
　Of their still waking jealousies, to raise
　Ourselves a fortune, by subverting theirs.
　We stand not in the lines, that do advance
　To that so courted point.

　　　　Enter SATRIUS and NATTA, at a distance.

Sil.
　But yonder lean
　A pair that do.

Sab. [salutes Latiaris.] Good cousin Latiaris.──

Sil.
　Satrius Secundus, and Pinnarius Natta,
　The great Sejanus' clients: there be two,
　Know more than honest counsels; whose close breasts,
　Were they ripp'd up to light, it would be found

A poor and idle sin, to which their trunks
Had not been made fit organs. These can lie,
Flatter, and swear, forswear, deprave, inform,
Smile, and betray; make guilty men; then beg
The forfeit lives, to get their livings; cut
Men's throats with whisperings; sell to gaping suitors
The empty smoke, that flies about the palace;
Laugh when their patron laughs; sweat when he sweats;
Be hot and cold with him; change every mood,
Habit, and garb, as often as he varies;
Observe him, as his watch observes his clock;
And, true, as turquoise in the dear lord's ring,
Look well or ill with him: 6 ready to praise
His lordship, if he spit, or but p—— fair,
Have an indifferent stool, or break wind well;
Nothing can 'scape their catch.

Sab.
Alas! these things
Deserve no note, conferr'd with other vile
And filthier flatteries, that corrupt the times;
When, not alone our gentries chief are fain
To make their safety from such sordid acts;
But all our consuls, and no little part
Of such as have been praetors, yea, the most
Of senators, that else not use their voices,
Start up in public senate and there strive
Who shall propound most abject things, and base.
So much, as oft Tuberous hath been heard,
Leaving the court, to cry, O race of men;
Prepared for servitude!——which shew'd that he.
Who least the public liberty could like,
As lothly brook'd their flat servility.

Sil.
Well, all is worthy of us, were it more,
Who with our riots, pride, and civil hate,
Have so provok'd the justice of the gods:
We, that, within these fourscore years, were born
Free, equal lords of the triumphed world,
And knew no masters, but affections;
To which betraying first our liberties,
We since became the slaves to one man's lusts;
And now to many: every minist'ring spy
That will accuse and swear, is lord of you,
Of me, of all our fortunes and our lives.
Our looks are call'd to question, and our words,
How innocent soever, are made crimes;
We shall not shortly dare to tell our dreams,

Or think, but 'twill be treason. Sab. Tyrants' arts
Are to give flatterers grace; accusers, power;
That those may seem to kill whom they devour.

Enter CORDUS and ARRUNTIUS.

Now, good Cremutius Cordus

Cor. [salutes Sabinus] Hail to your lordship!

Nat. [whispers Latiaris.] Who's that salutes your cousin?

Lat.
  'Tis one Cordus,
  A gentleman of Rome: one that has writ
  Annals of late, they say, and very well.

Nat. Annals! of what times?

Lat.
  I think of Pompey's,
  And Caius Caesar's; and so down to these.

Nat.
  How stands he affected to the present state!
  Is he or Drusian, or Germanic,
  Or ours, or neutral?

Lat. I know him not so far.

Nat.
  Those times are somewhat queasy to be touch'd.
  Have you or seen, or heard part of his work?

Lat. Not I; he means they shall be public shortly.

Nat. O, Cordus do you call him?

Lat. Ay.   [Exeunt Natta and Satrius

Sab.
  But these our times
  Are not the same, Arruntius.

Arr.
  Times! the men,
  The men are not the same: 'tis we are base,
  Poor, and degenerate from the exalted strain
  Of our great fathers. Where is now the soul

Of god-like Cato? he, that durst be good,
When Caesar durst be evil; and had power,
As not to live his slave, to die his master?
Or where's the constant Brutus, that being proof
Against all charm of benefits, did strike
So brave a blow into the monster's heart
That sought unkindly to captive his country?
O, they are fled the light! Those mighty spirits
Lie raked up with their ashes in their urns,
And not a spark of their eternal fire
Glows in a present bosom. All's but blaze,
Flashes and smoke, wherewith we labour so,
There's nothing Roman in us; nothing good,
Gallant, or great: 'tis true that Cordus says,
"Brave Cassius was the last of all that race."

    Drusus passes over the stage, attended by HATERIUS, etc.

Sab. Stand by! lord Drusus.

Hat. The emperor's son! give place.

Sil. I like the prince well.

Arr.
  A riotous youth;
  There's little hope of him.

Sab.
  That fault his age
  Will, as it grows, correct. Methinks he bears
  Himself each day more nobly than other;
  And wins no less on men's affections,
  Than doth his father lose. Believe me,
  I love him; And chiefly for opposing to Sejanus.

Sil.
  And I, for gracing his young kinsmen so,
  The sons of prince Germanicus: it shews
  A gallant clearness in him, a straight mind,
  That envies not, in them, their father's name.

Arr.
  His name was, while he lived, above all envy;
  And, being dead, without it. O, that man!
  If there were seeds of the old virtue left,
  They lived in him.

Sil.

  He had the fruits, Arruntius,
More than the seeds: Sabinus, and myself
Had means to know him within; and can report him.
We were his followers, he would call us friends;
He was a man most like to virtue; in all,
And every action, nearer to the gods,
Than men, in nature; of a body as fair
As was his mind; and no less reverend
In face, than fame: he could so use his state,
Tempering his greatness with his gravity,
As it avoided all self-love in him,
And spite in others. What his funerals lack'd
In images and pomp, they had supplied
With honourable sorrow, soldiers' sadness,
A kind of silent mourning, such, as men,
Who know no tears, but from their captives, use
To shew in so great losses.

Cor.
  I thought once,
Considering their forms, age, manner of deaths,
The nearness of the places where they fell,
To have parallel'd him with great Alexander:
For both were of best feature, of high race,
Year'd but to thirty, and, in foreign lands,
By their own people alike made away.
Sab, I know not, for his death, how you might wrest it:
But, for his life, it did as much disdain
Comparison, with that voluptuous, rash,
Giddy, and drunken Macedon's, as mine
Doth with my bondman's. All the good in him,
His valour and his fortune, he made his;
But he had other touches of late Romans,
That more did speak him: Pompey's dignity,
The innocence of Cato, Caesar's spirit,
Wise Brutus' temperance; and every virtue,
Which, parted unto others, gave them name,
Flow'd mix'd in him. He was the soul of goodness;
And all our praises of him are like streams
Drawn from a spring, that still rise full, and leave
The part remaining greatest.

Arr.
  I am sure
He was too great for us, and that they knew
Who did remove him hence.

Sab.
  When men grow fast

Honour'd and loved. there is a trick in state,
Which jealous princes never fail to use,
How to decline that growth, with fair pretext,
And honourable colours of employment,
Either by embassy, the war, or such,
To shift them forth into another air,
Where they may purge and lessen; so was he:
And had his seconds there, sent by Tiberius,
And his more subtile dam, to discontent him;
To breed and cherish mutinies; detract
His greatest actions; give audacious check
To his commands; and work to put him out
In open act of treason. All which snares
When his wise cares prevented, a fine poison
Was thought on, to mature their practices.

        Enter SEJANUS talking to TERENTIUS,
        followed by SATRIUS, NATTA, etc.

Cor. Here comes Sejanus.

Sil.
  Now observe the stoops,
The bendings, and the falls.

Arr. Most creeping base!

Sej. [to Natta.] I note them well: no more. Say you?

Sat.
  My lord,
There is a gentleman of Rome would buy-

Sej. How call you him you talk'd with?

Sat.
  Please your lordship,
It is Eudemus, the physician
to Livia, Drusus' wife.

Sej. On with your suit. Would buy, you said-

Sat. A tribune's place, my lord.

Sej. What will he give?

Sat. Fifty sestertia.

Sej. Livia's physician, say you, is that fellow?

Sat. It is, my lord: Your lordship's answer.

Sej.
   To what?

Sat.
   The place, my lord. 'Tis for a gentleman
   Your lordship will well like of, when you see him;
   And one, that you may make yours, by the grant.

Sej.
   Well, let him bring his money, and his name.

Sat.
   'Thank your lordship. He shall, my lord.

Sej.
   Come hither.
   Know you this same Eudemus? is he learn'd?

Sat.
   Reputed so, my lord, and of deep practice.

Sej.
   Bring him in, to me, in the gallery;
   And take you cause to leave us there together:
   I would confer with him, about a grief——
   On.   [Exeunt Sejanus, Satrius, Terentius, etc.

Arr.
   So! yet another? yet? O desperate state
   Of grovelling honour! seest thou this, O sun,
   And do we see thee after? Methinks, day
   Should lose his light, when men do lose their shames,
   And for the empty circumstance of life,
   Betray their cause of living.

Sil.
   Nothing so.
   Sejanus can repair, if Jove should ruin.
   He is now the court god; and well applied
   With sacrifice of knees, of crooks, and cringes;
   He will do more than all the house of heaven
   Can, for a thousand hecatombs. 'Tis he
   Makes us our day, or night; hell, and elysium
   Are in his look: we talk of Rhadamanth,
   Furies, and firebrands; but it is his frown
   That is all these; where, on the adverse part,

His smile is more, than e'er yet poets feign'd
Of bliss, and shades, nectar——

Arr.
A serving boy!
I knew him, at Caius' trencher, when for hire
He prostituted his abused body
To that great gormond, fat Apicius;
And was the noted pathic of the time.

Sab.
And, now, the second face of the whole world!
The partner of the empire, hath his image
Rear'd equal with Tiberius, born in ensigns;
Commands, disposes every dignity,
Centurions, tribunes, heads of provinces,
Praetors and consuls; all that heretofore
Rome's general suffrage gave, is now his sale.
The gain, or rather spoil of all the earth,
One, and his house, receives.

Sil.
He hath of late
Made him a strength too, strangely, by reducing
All the praetorian bands into one camp,
Which he commands: pretending that the soldiers,
By living loose and scatter'd, fell to riot;
And that if any sudden enterprise
Should be attempted, their united strength
Would be far more than sever'd; and their life
More strict, if from the city more removed.

Sab.
Where, now, he builds what kind of forts he please,
Is heard to court the soldier by his name,
Woos, feasts the chiefest men of action,
Whose wants, not loves, compel them to be his.
And though he ne'er were liberal by kind,
Yet to his own dark ends, he's most profuse,
Lavish, and letting fly, he cares not what
To his ambition.

Arr.
Yet, hath he ambition?
Is there that step in state can make him higher,
Or more, or anything he is, but less?

Sil. Nothing but emperor.

Arr.
　The name Tiberius,
　I hope, will keep, howe'er he hath foregone
　The dignity and power.

Sil. Sure, while he lives.

Arr.
　And dead, it comes to Drusus.
　Should he fail, To the brave issue of Germanicus;
　And they are three: too many-ha? for him
　To have a plot upon!

Sab.
　I do not know
　The heart of his designs; but, sure, their face
　Looks farther than the present.

Arr.
　By the gods,
　If I could guess he had but such a thought,
　My sword should cleave him down from head to heart,
　But I would find it out: and with my hand
　I'd hurl his panting brain about the air
　In mites, as small as atomi, to undo
　The knotted bed-

Sab. You are observ'd, Arruntius.

Arr. [turns to Natta, Terentius, etc.]
　Death! I dare tell him so; and all his spies:
　You, sir, I would, do you look? and you.

Sab. Forbear.
　　　　　　SCENE II.

(The former scene continued.)
A Gallery discovered opening into the state Room.
　　　Enter SATRIUS with EUDEMUS.

Sat.
　Here he will instant be: let's walk a turn;
　You're in a muse, Eudemus.

Eud.
　Not I, sir.
　I wonder he should mark me out so! well,
　Jove and Apollo form it for the best.　　　　[Aside.

Bat.
>Your fortune's made unto you now, Eudemus,
>If you can but lay bold upon the means;
>Do but observe his humour, and—believe it—
>He is the noblest Roman, where he takes——

> Enter SEJANUS.
>Here comes his lordship.

Sej. Now, good Satrius.

Sat. This is the gentleman, my lord.

Sej.
>Is this?
>Give me your hand—we must be more acquainted.
>Report, sir, hath spoke out your art and learning:
>And I am glad I have so needful cause,
>However in itself painful and hard,
>To make me known to so great virtue.——Look,
>Who is that, Satrius?   [Exit Sat.]
>   I have a grief, sir,
>That will desire your help. Your name's Eudemus!

Eud. Yes.

Sej. Sir?

Eud. It is, my lord.

Sej.
>I hear you are
>Physician to Livia, the princess.

Eud. I minister unto her, my good lord.

Sej. You minister to a royal lady, then.

Eud. She is, my, lord, and fair.

Sej.
>That's understood
>Of all her sex, who are or would be so;
>And those that would be, physic soon can make them:
>For those that are, their beauties fear no colours.

Eud. Your lordship is conceited.

Sej.

Sir, you know it,
And can, if need be, read a learned lecture
On this, and other secrets. 'Pray you, tell me,
What more of ladies besides Livia,
Have you your patients?

Eud.
Many, my good lord.
The great Augusta, Urgulania,
Mutilia Prisca, and Plancina; divers——

Sej.
And all these tell you the particulars
Of every several grief? how first it grew,
And then increased; what action caused that;
What passion that: and answer to each point
That you will put them?

Eud.
Else, my lord, we know not
How to prescribe the remedies.

Sej.
Go to,
you are a subtile nation, you physicians!
And grown the only cabinets in court,
To ladies' privacies. Faith, which of these
Is the most pleasant lady in her physic?
Come, you are modest now.

Eud. 'Tis fit, my lord.

Sej.
Why, sir, I do not-ask you of their urines,
Whose smell's most violet, or whose siege is best,
Or who makes hardest faces on her stool?
Which lady sleeps with her own face a nights?
Which puts her teeth off, with her clothes, in court?
Or, which her hair, which her complexion,
And, in which box she puts it; These were questions,
That might, perhaps, have put your gravity
To some defence of blush. But, I enquired,
Which was the wittiest, merriest, wantonnest? H
armless intergatories, but conceits.——
Methinks Augusta should be most perverse,
And froward in her fit.

Eud. She's so, my lord.

Sej. I knew it: and Mutilia the most jocund.

Eud. 'Tis very true, my lord.

Sej.
   And why would you
Conceal this from me, now? Come, what is Livia?
I know she's quick and quaintly spirited,
And will have strange thoughts, when she is at leisure:
She tells them all to you.

Eud.
   My noblest lord,
He breathes not in the empire, or on earth.
Whom I would be ambitious to serve
In any act, that may preserve mine honour,
Before your lordship.

Sej.
   Sir, you can lose no honour,
By trusting aught to me. The coarsest act
Done to my service, I can so requite,
As all the world shall style it honourable:
Your idle, virtuous definitions,
Keep honour poor, and are as scorn'd as vain:
Those deeds breathe honour that do suck in gain.

Eud.
   But, good my lord, if I should thus betray
The counsels of my patient, and a lady's
Of her high place and worth; what might your lordship,
Who presently are to trust me with your own,
Judge of my faith?

Sej.
   Only the best I swear.
Say now that I should utter you my grief,
And with it the true cause; that it were love,
And love to Livia; you should tell her this:
Should she suspect your faith; I would you could
Tell me as much from her; see if my brain
Could be turn'd jealous.

Eud.
   Happily, my lord,
I could in time tell you as much and more;
So I might safely promise but the first
To her from you.

Sej.
  As safely, my Eudemus,
  I now dare call thee so, as I have put
  The secret into thee.

Eud. My lord——

Sej.
  Protest not,
  Thy looks are vows to me; use only speed,
  And but affect her with Sejanus' love,
  Thou art a man, made to make consuls. Go.

Eud.
  My lord, I'll promise you a private meeting
  This day together.

Sej. Canst thou?

Eud. Yes.

Sej. The place?

Eud.
  My gardens, whither I shall fetch your lordship

Sej;
  Let me adore my AEsculapius.
  Why, this indeed is physic! and outspeaks
  The knowledge of cheap drugs, or any use
  Can be made out of it! more comforting
  Than all your opiates, juleps, apozems,
  Magistral syrups, or—— Be gone, my friend,
  Not barely styled, but created so;
  Expect things greater than thy largest hopes,
  To overtake thee: Fortune shall be taught
  To know how ill she hath deserv'd thus long,
  To come behind thy wishes. Go, and speed.   [Exit Eudemus.
  Ambition makes more trusty slaves than need.
  These fellows, by the favour of their art,
  Have still the means to tempt; oft-times the power.
  If Livia will be now corrupted, then
  Thou hast the way, Sejanus, to work out
  His secrets, who, thou know'st, endures thee not,
  Her husband, Drusus: and to work against them.
  Prosper it, Pallas, thou that better'st wit;
  For Venus hath the smallest share in it.
            Enter TIBERIUS and DRUSUS, attended.

Tib. [to Haterius, who kneels to him.]

    We not endure these flatteries; let him stand;
    Our empire, ensigns, axes, rods and state
    Take not away our human nature from us:
    Look up on us, and fall before the gods.

Sej. How like a god speaks Caesar!

Arr.
    There, observe!
    He can endure that second, that's no flattery.
    O, what is it, proud slime will not believe
    Of his own worth, to hear it equal praised
    Thus with the gods!

Oar. He did not hear it, sir.

Arr.
    He did not! Tut, he must not, we think meanly.
    'Tis your most courtly known confederacy,
    To have your private parasite redeem,
    What he, in public, subtilely will lose,
    To making him a name.

Hat. Right mighty lord——   [Gives him letters.

Tib.
    We must make up our ears 'gainst these assaults
    Of charming tongues; we pray you use no more
    These contumelies to us; style not us
    Or lord, or mighty, who profess ourself
    The servant of the senate, and are proud
    T' enjoy them our good, just, and favouring lords.

Car. Rarely dissembled!

Arr. Prince-like to the life.

Sab.
    When power that may command, so much descends,
    Their bondage, whom it stoops to, it intends.

Tib. Whence are these letters?

Hat. From the senate.

Tib. So.   [Lat. gives him letters.
    Whence these?

Lat. From thence too.

Tib. Are they sitting now?

Lat. They stay thy answer, Caesar.

Sil.
  If this man
  Had but a mind allied unto his words,
  How blest a fate were it to us, and Rome!
  We could not think that state for which to change,
  Although the aim were our old liberty:
  The ghosts of those that fell for that, would grieve
  Their bodies lived not, now, again to serve.
  Men are deceived, who think there can be thrall
  Beneath a virtuous prince: Wish'd liberty
  Ne'er lovelier looks, than under such a crown.
  But, when his grace is merely but lip-good,
  And that, no longer than he airs himself
  Abroad in public, there, to seem to shun
  The strokes and stripes of flatterers, which within
  Are lechery unto him, and so feed
  His brutish sense with their afflicting sound,
  As, dead to virtue, he permits himself
  Be carried like a pitcher by the ears,
  To every act of vice: this is the case
  Deserves our fear, and doth presage the nigh
  And close approach of blood and tyranny.
  Flattery is midwife unto prince's rage:
  And nothing sooner doth help forth a tyrant,
  Than that and whisperers' grace, who have the time,
  The place, the power, to make all men offenders.

Arr.
  He should be told this; and be bid dissemble
  With fools and blind men: we that know the evil,
  Should hunt the palace-rats or give them bane;
  Fright hence these worse than ravens, that devour T
  he quick, where they but prey upon the dead:
  He shall be told it.

Sab.
  Stay, Arruntius,
  We must abide our opportunity;
  And practise what is fit, as what is needful.
  It is not safe t' enforce a sovereign's ear:
  Princes hear well, if they at all will hear.

Arr.
  Ha, say you so? well! In the mean time, Jove,

(Say not, but I do call upon thee now,)

Sil. 'Tis well pray'd.

Tib. [having read the letters.]
　Return the lords this voice,——
　We are their creature,
　And it is fit a good and honest prince,
　Whom they, out of their bounty, have instructed
　With so dilate and absolute a power,
　Should owe the office of it to their service.
　And good of all and every citizen.
　Nor shall it e'er repent us to have wish'd
　The senate just, and favouring lords unto us,
　Since their free loves do yield no less defence
　To a prince's state, than his own innocence.
　Say then, there can be nothing in their thought
　Shall want to please us, that hath pleased them;
　Our suffrage rather shall prevent than stay
　Behind their wills: 'tis empire to obey,
　Where such, so great, so grave, so good determine.
　Yet, for the suit of Spain, to erect a temple
　In honour of our mother and our self,
　We must, with pardon of the senate, not
　Assent thereto. Their lordships may object
　Our not denying the same late request
　Unto the Asian cities: we desire
　That our defence for suffering that be known
　In these brief reasons, with our after purpose.
　Since deified Augustus hindered not
　A temple to be built at Pergamum,
　In honour of himself and sacred Rome;
　We, that have all his deeds and words observed
　Ever, in place of laws, the rather follow'd
　That pleasing precedent, because with ours,
　The senate's reverence, also, there was join'd.
　But as, t' have once received it, may deserve
　The gain of pardon; so, to be adored
　With the continued style, and note of gods,
　Through all the provinces, were wild ambition.
　And no less pride: yea, even Augustus' name
　Would early vanish, should it be profaned
　With such promiscuous flatteries. For our part,
　We here protest it, and are covetous
　Posterity should know it. we are mortal;
　And can but deeds of men: 'twere glory enough,
　Could we be truly a prince. And, they shall add
　Abounding grace unto our memory,
　That shall report us worthy our forefathers,

    Careful of your affairs, constant in dangers,
    And not afraid of any private frown
    For public good. These things shall be to us
    Temples and statues, reared in your minds,
    The fairest, and most during imagery:
    For those of stone or brass, if they become
    Odious in judgment of posterity,
    Are more contemn'd as dying sepulchres,
    Than ta'en for living monuments. We then
    Make here our suit, alike to gods and men;
    The one, until the period of our race,
    To inspire us with a free and quiet mind,
    Discerning both divine and human laws;
    The other, to vouchsafe us after death,
    An honourable mention, and fair praise,
    To accompany our actions and our name:
    The rest of greatness princes may command,
    And, therefore, may neglect; only, a long,
    A lasting, high, and happy memory
    They should, without being satisfied, pursue:
    Contempt of fame begets contempt of virtue.

Nat. Rare!

Bat. Most divine!

Sej.
    The oracles are ceased,
    That only Caesar, with their tongue, might speak.

Arr. Let me be gone: most felt and open this!

Cor. Stay.

Arr.
    What! to hear more cunning and fine words,
    With their sound flatter'd ere their sense be meant?

Tib.
    Their choice of Antium, there to place the gift
    Vow'd to the goddess for our mother's health,
    We will the senate know, we fairly like:
    As also of their grant to Lepidus,
    For his repairing the AEmilian place,
    And restoration of those monuments:
    Their grace too in confining of Silanus
    To the other isle Cithera, at the suit
    Of his religious sister, much commends
    Their policy, so temper'd with their mercy.

But for the honours which they have decreed
To our Sejanus, to advance his statue
In Pompey's theatre, (whose ruining fire
His vigilance and labour kept restrain'd
In that one loss,) they have therein out-gone
Their own great wisdoms, by their skilful choice,
And placing of their bounties on a man,
Whose merit more adorns the dignity,
Than that can him; and gives a benefit,
In taking, greater than it can receive.
Blush not, Sejanus, thou great aid of Rome,
Associate of our labours, our chief helper;
Let us not force thy simple modesty
With offering at thy praise, for more we cannot,
Since there's no voice can take it.
No man here Receive our speeches as hyperboles:
For we are far from flattering our friend,
Let envy know, as from the need to flatter.
Nor let them ask the causes of our praise:
Princes have still their grounds rear'd with themselves,
Above the poor low flats of common men;
And who will search the reasons of their acts,
Must stand on equal bases. Lead, away:
Our loves unto the senate.
    [Exeunt Tib., Sejan., Natta, Hat., Lat., Officers, etc.

Arr. Caesar!

Sab. Peace.

Cor.
  Great Pompey's theatre was never ruin'd
  Till now, that proud Sejanus hath a statue
  Rear'd on his ashes.

Arr.
  Place the shame of soldiers,
  Above the best of generals? crack the world,
  And bruise the name of Romans into dust,
  Ere we behold it!

Sil. Check your passion; Lord Drusus tarries.

Dru.
  Is my father mad,
  Weary of life, and rule, lords? thus to heave
  An idol up with praise! make him his mate,
  His rival in the empire!

Arr. O, good prince.

Dru.
  Allow him statues, titles, honours, such
  As he himself refuseth!

Arr. Brave, brave Drusus!

Dru.
  The first ascents to sovereignty are hard;
  But, entered once, there never wants or means,
  Or ministers, to help the aspirer on.

Arr. True, gallant Drusus.

Dru.
  We must shortly pray
  To Modesty, that he will rest contented——

Arr.
  Ay, where he is, and not write emperor.

        Re-enter SEJANUS, SATBIUS, LATIARIS, Clients, etc.

Sej.
  There is your bill, and yours; bring you your man.
                        [To Satrius.
  I have moved for you, too, Latiaris.

Dru.
  What!
  Is your vast greatness grown so blindly bold,
  That you will over us?

Sej. Why then give way.

Dru.
  Give way, Colossus! do you lift? advance you?
  Take that!   [Strikes him.

Arr. Good! brave! excellent, brave prince!

Dru. Nay, come, approach.   [Draws his sword.
        What, stand you off? at gaze?
  It looks too full of death for thy cold spirits.
  Avoid mine eye, dull camel, or my sword
  Shall make thy bravery fitter for a grave,
  Than for a triumph. I'll advance a statue
  O' your own bulk; but 't shall be on the cross;
  Where I will nail your pride at breadth and length,

    And crack those sinews, which are yet but stretch'd
    With your swoln fortune's rage.

Arr. A noble prince!

All. A Castor, a Castor, a Castor, a Castor!
                        [Exeunt all but Sejanus.
Sej.
    He that, with such wrong moved, can bear it through
    With patience, and an even mind, knows how
    To turn it back. Wrath cover'd carries fate:
    Revenge is lost, if I profess my hate.
    What was my practice late, I'll now pursue,
    As my fell justice: this hath styled it new.   [Exit.

ACT II

SCENE I.——The Garden of EUDEMUS.
Enter SEJANUS, LIVIA, and EUDEMUS.

Sej.
  Physician, thou art worthy of a province.
  For the great favours done unto our loves;
  And, but that greatest Livia bears a part
  In the requital of thy services,
  I should alone despair of aught, like means,
  To give them worthy satisfaction.

Liv.
  Eudemus, I will see it, shall receive
  A fit and full reward for his large merit.——
  But for this potion we intend to Drusus,
  No more our husband now, whom shall we choose
  As the most apt and able instrument,
  To minister it to him?

Eud. I say, Lygdus.

Sej. Lygdus what's he?

Liv. An eunuch Drusus loves.

Eud. Ay, and his cup-bearer.

Sej.
  Name not a second.
  If Drusus love him, and he have that place,
  We cannot think a fitter.

Eud.
  True, my lord.
  For free access and trust are two main aids.

Sej. Skilful physician!

Liv.
  But he must be wrought
  To the undertaking, with some labour'd art.

Sej. Is he ambitious?

Liv. No.

Sej. Or covetous?

Liv. Neither.

Eud. Yet, gold is a good general charm.

Sej. What is he, then?

Liv. Faith, only wanton, light.

Sej. How! is he young and fair?

Eud. A delicate youth.

Sej.
  Send him to me, I'll work him.——Royal lady,
Though I have loved you long, and with that height
Of zeal and duty, like the fire, which more
It mounts it trembles, thinking nought could add
Unto the fervour which your eye had kindled;
Yet, now I see your wisdom, judgment, strength,
Quickness, and will, to apprehend the means
To your own good and greatness, I protest
Myself through rarified, and turn'd all flame
In your affection: such a spirit as yours,
Was not created for the idle second
To a poor flash, as Drusus; but to shine
Bright as the moon among the lesser lights,
And share the sov'reignty of all the world.
Then Livia triumphs in her proper sphere,
When she and her Sejanus shall divide
The name of Caesar, and Augusta's star
Be dimm'd with glory of a brighter beam:
When Agrippina's fires are quite extinct,
And the scarce-soon Tiberius borrows all
His little light from us, whose folded arms
Shall make one perfect orb.   [Knocking within.]
Who's that! Eudemus, Look.   [Exit Eudemus.]
'Tis not Drusus, lady, do not fear.

Liv.
  Not I, my lord: my fear and love of him
Left me at once.

Sej. Illustrious lady, stay——

Eud. [within.] I'll tell his lordship.   [Re-enter EUDEMUS.

Sej. Who is it, Eudemus?

Eud.
>One of your lordship's servants brings you word
>The emperor hath sent for you.

Sej.
>O! where is he?
>With your fair leave, dear princess, I'll but ask
>A question and return.   [Exit.

Eud.
>Fortunate princess!
>How are you blest in the fruition
>Of this unequall'd man, the soul of Rome,
>The empire's life, and voice of Caesar's world!

Liv.
>So blessed, my Eudemus, as to know
>The bliss I have, with what I ought to owe
>The means that wrought it. How do I look to-day?

Eud.
>Excellent clear, believe it. This same fucus
>Was well laid on.

Liv. Methinks 'tis here not white.

Eud.
>Lend me your scarlet, lady. 'Tis the sun,
>Hath giv'n some little taint unto the ceruse;
>You should have used of the white oil I gave you.
>Sejanus, for your love! his very name
>Commandeth above Cupid or his shafts——   [Paints her cheeks.

Liv. Nay, now you've made it worse.

Eud.
>I'll help it straight——
>And but pronounced, is a sufficient charm
>Against all rumour; and of absolute power
>To satisfy for any lady's honour.

Liv. What do you now, Eudemus?

Eud.
>Make a light fucus,
>To touch you o'er withal.——Honour'd Sejanus!
>What act, though ne'er so strange and insolent,
>But that addition will at least bear out,
>If't do not expiate?

Liv. Here, good physician.

Eud.
  I like this study to preserve the love
  Of such a man, that comes not every hour
  To greet the world.-'Tis now well, lady, you should
  Use of the dentifrice I prescribed you too,
  To clear your teeth, and the prepared pomatum,
  To smooth the skin:——A lady cannot be
  Too curious of her form, that still would hold
  The heart of such a person, made her captive,
  As you have his: who, to endear him more
  In your clear eye, hath put away his wife,
  The trouble of his bed, and your delights,
  Fair Apicata, and made spacious room
  To your new pleasures.

Liv.
  Have not we return'd
  That with our hate to Drusus, and discovery
  Of all his counsels?

Eud.
  Yes, and wisely, lady.
  The ages that succeed, and stand far off
  To gaze at your high prudence, shall admire,
  And reckon it an act without your sex:
  It hath that rare appearance. Some will think
  Your fortune could not yield a deeper sound,
  Than mix'd with Drusus; but, when they shall hear
  That, and the thunder of Sejanus meet,
  Sejanus, whose high name doth strike the stars,
  And rings about the concave; great Sejanus,
  Whose glories, style, and titles are himself,
  The often iterating of Sejanus:
  They then will lose their thoughts, and be ashamed
  To take acquaintance of them.
                    Be-enter SEJANUS.
Sej.
  I must make
  A rude departure, lady: Caesar sends
  With all his haste both of command and prayer.
  Be resolute in our plot; you have my soul,
  As certain yours as it is my body's.
  And, wise physician, so prepare the poison,
  As you may lay the subtile operation
  Upon some natural disease of his:
  Your eunuch send to me. I kiss your hands,

Glory of ladies, and commend my love
To your best faith and memory.

Liv.
My lord,
I shall but change your words. Farewell.
Yet, this Remember for your heed, he loves you not;
You know what I have told you: his designs
Are full of grudge and danger; we must use
More than a common speed.

Sej.
Excellent lady,
How you do fire my blood!

Liv.
Well, you must go?
The thoughts be best, are least set forth to shew.
                                 [Exit Sejanus.

Eud. When will you take some physic, lady?

Liv.
When
I shall, Eudemus: but let Drusus' drug
Be first prepared.

Eud.
Were Lygdus made, that's done;
I have it ready. And to-morrow morning
I'll send you a perfume, first to resolve
And procure sweat, and then prepare a bath
To cleanse and clear the cutis; against when
I'll have an excellent new fucus made,
Resistive 'gainst the sun, the rain, or wind,
Which you shall lay on with a breath, or oil,
As you best like, and last some fourteen hours.
This change came timely, lady, for your health,
And the restoring your complexion,
Which Drusus' choler had almost burnt up!
Wherein your fortune hath prescribed you better
Than art could do.

Liv.
Thanks, good physician,
I'll use my fortune, you shall see, with reverence.
Is my coach ready?

Eud. It attends your highness.   [Exeunt

SCENE II.——An Apartment in the Palace.
Enter SEJANUS.

Sej.
  If this be not revenge, when I have done
  And made it perfect, let Egyptian slaves,
  Parthians, and bare-foot Hebrews brand my face,
  And print my body full of injuries.
  Thou lost thyself, child Drusus, when thou thoughtst
  Thou couldst outskip my vengeance; or outstand
  The power I had to crush thee into air.
  Thy follies now shall taste what kind of man
  They have provoked, and this thy father's house
  Crack in the flame of my incensed rage,
  Whose fury shall admit no shame or mean.——
  Adultery! it is the lightest ill
  I will commit A race of wicked acts
  Shall flow out of my anger, and o'erspread
  The world's wide face, which no posterity
  Shall e'er approve, nor yet keep silent: things
  That for their cunning, close, and cruel mark,
  Thy father would wish his: and shall, perhaps,
  Carry the empty name, but we the prize.
  On, then, my soul, and start not in thy course;
  Though heaven drop sulphur, and hell belch out fire,
  Laugh at the idle terrors; tell proud Jove,
  Between his power and thine there is no odds:
  'Twas only fear first in the world made gods!
              Enter TIBERIUS, attended.

Tib. Is yet Sejanus come?

Sej. He's here, dread Caesar.

Tib.
  Let all depart that chamber, and the next.
                  [Exeunt Attendants.
  Sit down, my comfort. When the master prince
  Of all the world, Sejanus, saith he fears, Is it not fatal?

Sewj. Yes, to those are fear'd.

Tib. And not to him?

Sej.
  Not, if he wisely turn
  That part of fate he holdeth, first on them.

Tib. That nature, blood, and laws of kind forbid.

Sej. Do policy and state forbid it?

Tib. No.

Sej.
   The rest of poor respects, then, let go by;
   State is enough to make the act just, them guilty.

Tib. Long hate pursues such acts.

Sej.
   Whom hatred frights,
   Let him not dream of sovereignty.

Tib.
   Are rites
   Of faith, love, piety, to be trod down,
   Forgotten, and made vain?

Sej.
   All for a crown.
   The prince who shames a tyrant's name to bear,
   Shall never dare do any thing, but fear;
   All the command of sceptres quite doth perish,
   If it begin religious thoughts to cherish:
   Whole empires fall, sway'd by those nice respects;
   It is the license of dark deeds protects
   Ev'n states most hated, when no laws resist
   The sword. but that it acteth what it list.

Tib.
   Yet so, we may do all things cruelly,
   Not safely.

Sej. Yes, and do them thoroughly.

Tib. Knows yet Sejanus whom we point at?

Sej.
   Ay,
   Or else my thought, my sense, or both do err:
   'Tis Agrippina.

Tib. She, and her proud race.

Sej.
   Proud! dangerous, Caesar: for in them apace
   The father's spirit shoots up. Germanicus
   Lives in their looks, their gait, their form, t' upbraid us

  With his close death, if not revenge the same.

Tib. The act's not known.

Sej.
 Not proved: but whispering Fame
 Knowledge and proof doth to the jealous give,
 Who, than to fail, would their own thought believe.
 It is not safe, the children draw long breath,
 That are provoked by a parent's death.

Tib.
 It is as dangerous to make them hence,
 If nothing but their birth be their offence.

Sej.
 Stay, till they strike at Caesar; then their crime
 Will be enough; but late and out of time For him to punish.

Tib. Do they purpose it?

Sej.
 You know, sir, thunder speaks not till it hit.
 Be not secure; none swiftlier are opprest,
 Than they whom confidence betrays to rest.
 Let not your daring make your danger such:
 All power is to be fear'd, where 'tis too much.
 The youths are of themselves hot, violent,
 Full of great thought; and that male-spirited dame,
 Their mother, slacks no means to put them on,
 By large allowance, popular presentings,
 Increase of train and state, suing for titles;
 Hath them commended with like prayers, like vows,
 To the same gods, with Caesar: days and nights
 She spends in banquets and ambitious feasts
 For the nobility; where Caius Silius,
 Titius Sabinus, old Arruntius,
 Asinius Gallus, Furnius, Regulus,
 And others of that discontented list,
 Are the prime guests. There, and to these, she tells
 Whose niece she was, whose daughter, and whose wife.
 And then must they compare her with Augusta,
 Ay, and prefer her too; commend her form,
 Extol her fruitfulness; at which a shower
 Falls for the memory of Germanicus,
 Which they blow over straight with windy praise,
 And puffing hopes of her aspiring sons;
 Who, with these hourly ticklings, grow so pleased,
 And wantonly conceited of themselves,

As now, they stick not to believe they're such
As these do give them out; and would be thought
More than competitors, immediate heirs.
Whilst to their thirst of rule, they win the rout
(That's still the friend of novelty) with hope
Of future freedom, which on every change
That greedily, though emptily expects.
Caesar, 'tis age in all things breeds neglects,
And princes that will keep old dignity
Must not admit too youthful heirs stand by;
Not their own issue; but so darkly set
As shadows are in picture, to give height
And lustre to themselves.

Tib.
    We will command
Their rank thoughts down, and with a stricter hand
Than we have yet put forth; their trains must bate,
Their titles, feasts, and factions.

Sej.
    Or your state.
But how, sir, will you work!

Tib. Confine them.

Sej.
    No.
They are too great, and that too faint a blow
To give them now; it would have serv'd at first,
When with the weakest touch their knot had burst.
But, now, your care must be, not to detect
The smallest cord, or line of your suspect;
For such, who know the weight of prince's fear,
Will, when they find themselves discover'd, rear
Their forces, like seen snakes, that else would lie
Roll'd in their circles, close: nought is more high,
Daring, or desperate, than offenders found;
Where guilt is, rage and courage both abound.
The course must be, to let them still swell up,
Riot, and surfeit on blind fortune's cup;
Give them more place, more dignities, more style,
Call them to court, to senate; in the while,
Take from their strength some one or twain, or more,
Of the main factors, (it will fright the store,)
And, by some by-occasion. Thus, with slight
You shall disarm them first; and they, in night
Of their ambition, not perceive the train,
Till in the engine they are caught and slain.

Tib.
  We would not kill, if we knew how to save;
  Yet, than a throne, 'tis cheaper give a grave.
  Is there no way to bind them by deserts?

Sej.
  Sir, wolves do change their hair, but not their hearts.
  While thus your thought unto a mean is tied,
  You neither dare enough, nor do provide.
  All modesty is fond: and chiefly where
  The subject is no less compell'd to bear,
  Than praise his sovereign's acts.

Tib.
  We can no longer
  Keep on our mask to thee, our dear Sejanus;
  Thy thoughts are ours, in all, and we but proved
  Their voice, in our designs, which by assenting
  Hath more confirm'd us, than if beart'ning Jove
  Had, from his hundred statues, bid us strike,
  And at the stroke click'd all his marble thumbs.
  But who shall first be struck?

Sej.
  First Caius Silius;
  He is the most of mark, and most of danger:
  In power and reputation equal strong,
  Having commanded an imperial army
  Seven years together, vanquish'd Sacrovir
  In Germany, and thence obtain'd to wear
  The ornaments triumphal. His steep fall,
  By how much it doth give the weightier crack,
  Will send more wounding terror to the rest,
  Command them stand aloof, and give more way
  To our surprising of the principal.

Tib. But what, Sabinus?

Sej.
  Let him grow a while,
  His fate is not yet ripe: we must not pluck
  At all together, lest we catch ourselves.
  And there's Arruntius too, he only talks.
  But Sosia, Silius' wife, would be wound in
  Now, for she hath a fury in her breast,
  More than hell ever knew; and would be sent
  Thither in time. Then is there one Cremutius
  Cordus, a writing fellow, they have got

To gather notes of the precedent times,
And make them into Annals; a most tart
And bitter spirit, I hear; who, under colour
Of praising those, doth tax the present state,
Censures the men, the actions, leaves no trick,
No practice unexamined, parallels
The times, the governments; a profest champion
For the old liberty-

Tib.
A perishing wretch!
As if there were that chaos bred in things,
That laws and liberty would not rather choose
To be quite broken, and ta'en hence by us,
Than have the stain to be preserved by such.
Have we the means to make these guilty first?
Sej.
Trust that to me: let Caesar, by his power
But cause a formal meeting of the senate,
I will have matter and accusers ready.

Tib. But how? let us consult.

Sej.
We shall misspend
The time of action. Counsels are unfit
In business, where all rest is more pernicious
Than rashness can be. Acts of this close kind
Thrive more by execution than advice.
There is no lingering in that work begun,
Which cannot praised be, until through done.

Tib.
Our edicts shall forthwith command a court.
While I can live, I will prevent earth's fury:
                    [Exit

Enter JULIUS POSTHUMUS.

Pos. My lord Sejanus——

Sej.
Julius Posthumus!
Come with my wish! What news from Agrippina's?

Pos.
Faith, none. They all lock up themselves a' late,
Or talk in character; I have not seen
A company so changed. Except they had

    Intelligence by augury of our practice.———

Sej. When were you there?

Pos. Last night.

Sej. And what guests found you?

Pos. Sabinus, Silius, the old list, Arruntius, Furmus, and Gallus.

Sej. Would not these talk?

Pos.
    Little:
And yet we offer'd choice of argument. Satrius was with me.

Sej.
    Well: 'tis guilt enough
Their often meeting. You forgot to extol
The hospitable lady?

Pas.
    No; that trick
Was well put home, and had succeeded too,
But that Sabinus cough'd a caution out;
For she began to swell.

Sej.
    And may she burst!
Julius, I would have you go instantly
Unto the palace of the great Augusta,
And, by your kindest friend, get swift access;
Acquaint her with these meetings: tell the words
You brought me the other day, of Silius,
Add somewhat to them. Make her understand
The danger of Sabinus, and the times,
Out of his closeness. Give Arruntius' words
Of malice against Caesar; so, to Gallus:
But, above all, to Agrippina. Say,
As you may truly, that her infinite pride,
Propt with the hopes of her too fruitful womb,
With popular studies gapes for sovereignty,
And threatens Caesar. Pray Augusta then,
That for her own, great Caesar's, and the public
safety, she be pleased to urge these dangers.
Caesar is too secure, he must be told,
And best he'll take it from a mother's tongue.
Alas! what is't for us to sound, to explore,
To watch, oppose, plot, practise, or prevent,

If he, for whom it is so strongly labour'd,
Shall, out of greatness and free spirit, be
Supinely negligent? our city's now
Divided as in time o' the civil war,
And men forbear not to declare themselves
Of Agrippina's party. Every day
The faction multiplies; and will do more,
If not resisted: you can best enlarge it,
As you find audience. Noble Posthumus,
Commend me to your Prisca: and pray her,
She will solicit this great business,
To earnest and most present execution,
With all her utmost credit with Augusta.

Pos. I shall not fail in my instructions.   [Exit.

Sej.
  This second, from his mother, will well urge
  Our late design, and spur on Caesar's rage;
  Which else might grow remiss. The way to put
  A prince in blood, is to present the shapes
  Of dangers, greater than they are, like late,
  Or early shadows; and, sometimes, to feign
  Where there are none, only to make him fear?
  His fear will make him cruel: and once enter'd,
  He doth not easily learn to stop, or spare
  Where he may doubt. This have I made my rule,
  To thrust Tiberius into tyranny,
  And make him toil, to turn aside those blocks,
  Which I alone could not remove with safety,
  Drusus once gone, Germanicus' three sons
  Would clog my way; whose guards have too much faith
  To be corrupted: and their mother known
  Of too, too unreproved a chastity,
  To be attempted, as light Livia was.
  Work then, my art, on Caesar's fears, as they
  On those they fear 'till all my lets be clear'd,
  And he in ruins of his house, and hate
  Of all his subjects, bury his own state;
  When with my peace and safety, I will rise,
  By making him the public sacrifice.   [Exit.
        SCENE III.-A Room in AGRIPPINA'S House.
            Enter SATRIUS and NATTA.
Sat. They're grown exceeding circumspect, and wary.

Nat.
  They have us in the wind: and yet Arruntius
  Cannot contain himself.

39

Sat.
   Tut, he's not yet
   Look'd after; there are others more desired
   That are more silent.

Nat. Here he comes. Away. [Exeunt.

   Enter SABINUS, ARRUNTIUS, and CORDUS

Sab.
   How is it, that these beagles haunt the house
   Of Agrippina?

Arr.
   O, they hunt, they hunt!
   There is some game here lodged, which they must rouse,
   To make the great ones sport.

Cor.
   Did you observe
   How they inveigh'd 'gainst Caesar?

Arr.
   Ay, baits, baits,
   For us to bite at: would I have my flesh
   Torn by the public hook, these qualified hangmen
   Should be my company.

Cor. Here comes another. [Dom. Afer passes over the stage

Arr.
   Ay, there's a man, Afer the orator!
   One that hath phrases, figures, and fine flowers,
   To strew his rhetoric with, and doth make haste,
   To get him note, or name, by any offer
   Where blood or gain be objects; steeps his words,
   When he would kill, in artificial tears:
   The crocodile of Tyber! him I love,
   That man is mine; he hath my heart and voice
   When I would curse! he, he.

Sub.
   Contemn the slaves,
   Their present lives will be their future graves. [Exeunt
       SCENE IV.-Another Apartment in the same.
       Enter SILIUS, AGRIPPINA, NERO, and SOSIA.

Sil.
   May't please your highness not forget yourself;

I dare not, with my manners, to attempt
Your trouble farther.

Agr. Farewell, noble Silius!

Sil. Most royal princess.

Agr. Sosia stays with us?

Sil.
She is your servant, and doth owe your grace
An honest, but unprofitable love.

Agr. How can that be, when there's no gain but virtue's?

Sil:
You take the moral, not the politic sense.
I meant, as she is bold, and free of speech,
Earnest to utter what her zealous thought
Travails withal, in honour of your house;
Which act, as it is simply born in her,
Partakes of love and honesty; but may,
By the over-often, and unseason'd use,
Turn to your loss and danger: for your state
Is waited on by envies, as by eyes;
And every second guest your tables take
Is a fee'd spy, to observe who goes, who comes;
What conference you have, with whom, where, when.
What the discourse is, what the looks, the thoughts
Of every person there, they do extract,
And make into a substance.

Agr.
Hear me, Silius.
Were all Tiberius' body stuck with eyes,
And every wall and hanging in my house
Transparent, AS this lawn I wear, or air;
Yea, had Sejanus both his ears as long
As to my inmost closet, I would hate
To whisper any thought, or change an act,
To be made Juno's rival. Virtue's forces
Shew ever noblest in conspicuous courses.

Sil.
'Tis great, and bravely spoken, like the spirit
Of Agrippina: yet, your highness knows,
There is nor loss nor shame in providence;
Few can, what all should do, beware enough.
You may perceive with what officious face,

Satrius, and Natta, Afer, and the rest.
Visit your house, of late, to enquire the secrets;
And with what bold and privileged art, they rail
Against Augusta, yea, and at Tiberius;
Tell tricks of Livia, and Sejanus; all
To excite, and call your indignation on,
That they might hear it at more liberty.

Agr. You're too suspicious, Silius.

Sil.
  Pray the gods,
  I be so, Agrippina; but I fear
  Some subtle practice. They that durst to strike
  At so exampless, and unblamed a life,
  As that of the renowned Germanicus,
  Will not sit down with that exploit alone:
  He threatens many that hath injured one.

Nero.
  'Twere best rip forth their tongues, sear out their eyes.
  When next they come.

Sos. A fit reward for spies.
                    Enter Drusus, jun.
Dru. jun. Hear you the rumour?

Agr. What?

Dru. jun. Drusus is dying.

Agr. Dying!

Nero. That's strange!

Agr. You were with him yesternight.

Dru. jun.
  One met Eudemus the physician,
  Sent for, but now; who thinks he cannot live.

Sil.
  Thinks! if it be arrived at that, he knows,
  Or none.

Agr. 'Tis quick! what should be his disease?

Sil. Poison, poison–

Agr. How, Silius!

Nero. What's that?

Sil.
  Nay, nothing. There was late a certain blow
  Given o' the face.

Nero. Ay, to Sejanus.

Sil. True!

Dru. jun. And what of that?

Sil. I'm glad I gave it not.

Nero. But there is somewhat else?

Sil.
  Yes, private meetings,
  With a great lady [sir], at a physician's,
  And a wife turn'd away.

Nero. Ha!

Sil.
  Toys, mere toys:
  What wisdom's now in th' streets, in the common mouth?

Dru. fun.
  Fears, whisperings, tumults, noise,
  I know not what: They say the Senate sit.

Sil.
  I'll thither straight;
  And see what's in the forge.

Agr. Good Silius do; Sosia and I will in.

Sil.
  Haste you, my lords, I
  To visit the sick prince; tender your loves,
  And sorrows to the people. This Sejanus,
  Trust my divining soul, hath plots on all:
  No tree, that stops his prospect, but must fall.   [Exeunt.

ACT III

SCENE I.-The Senate-House
Enter Praenes, Lictores, SEJANUS, VARRO, LATIARIS, COTTA, and AFER

Sej.
'Tis only you must urge against him, Varro;
Nor I nor Caesar may appear therein,
Except in your defence, who are the consul;
And, under colour of late enmity
Between your father and his, may better do it,
As free from all suspicion of a practice.
Here be your notes, what points to touch at; read:
Be cunning in them. Afer has them too.

Var. But is he summon'd?

Sej.
No. It was debated
By Caesar, and concluded as most fit
To take him unprepared.

Afer.
And prosecute
All under name of treason.

Var. I conceive.
Enter SABINUS, GALLUS, LEPIDUS, and ARRUNTIUS.
Sab. Drusus being dead, Caesar will not be here.

Gal. What should the business of this senate be?

Arr.
That can my subtle whisperers tell you: we
That are the good-dull-noble lookers on,
Are only call'd to keep the marble warm.
What should we do with those deep mysteries,
Proper to these fine heads? let them alone.
Our ignorance may, perchance, help us be saved
From whips and furies.

Gall. See, see, see their action!

Arr.
Ay, now their heads do travail, now they work;
Their faces run like shittles; they are weaving
Some curious cobweb to catch flies.

Sab.
  Observe,
  They take their places.

Arr. What, so low!

Gal.
  O yes,
  They must be seen to flatter Caesar's grief,
  Though but in sitting.

Var. Bid us silence.

Prae. Silence!

Var.
  Fathers conscript, may this our present meeting,
  Turn fair, and fortunate to the common-wealth!
                    Enter SILIUS, and other Senators.
Sej. See, Silius enters.

Sil. Hail, grave fathers!

Lic.
  Stand.
  Silius, forbear thy place.

Ben. How!

Prae.
  Silius, stand forth,
  The consul hath to charge thee.

Lic. Room for Caesar.

Arr. Is he come too! nay then expect a trick.

Sab. Silius accused! sure he will answer nobly.
                    Enter TIBERIUS, attended.
Tib.
  We stand amazed, fathers, to behold
  This general dejection. Wherefore sit
  Rome's consuls thus dissolved, as they had lost
  All the remembrance both of style and place
  It not becomes. No woes are of fit weight,
  To make the honour of the empire stoop:
  Though I, in my peculiar self, may meet
  Just reprehension, that so suddenly,

And, in so fresh a grief, would greet the senate,
When private tongues, of kinsmen and allies,
Inspired with comforts, lothly are endured,
The face of men not seen, and scarce the day,
To thousands that communicate our loss.
Nor can I argue these of weakness; since
They take but natural ways; yet I must seek
For stronger aids, and those fair helps draw out
From warm embraces of the common-wealth.
Our mother, great Augusta, 's struck with time,
Our self imprest with aged characters,
Drusus is gone, his children young and babes;
Our aims must now reflect on those that may
Give timely succour to these present ills,
And are our only glad-surviving hopes,
The noble issue of Germanicus,
Nero and Drusus: might it please the consul
Honour them in, they both attend without.
I would present them to the senate's care,
And raise those suns of joy that should drink up
These floods of sorrow in your drowned eyes.

Arr.
  By Jove, I am not OEdipus enough
  To understand this Sphynx.

Sab. The princes come.
                    Enter NERO, and DRUSUS, junior.
Tib.
  Approach you, noble Nero, noble Drusus.
These princes, fathers, when their parent died,
I gave unto their uncle, with this prayer,
That though he had proper issue of his own,
He would no less bring up, and foster these,
Than that self-blood; and by that act confirm
Their worths to him, and to posterity.
Drusus ta'en hence, I turn my prayers to you,
And 'fore our country, and our gods, beseech
You take, and rule Augustus' nephew's sons,
Sprung of the noblest ancestors; and so
Accomplish both my duty, and your own,
Nero, and Drusus, these shall be to you
In place of parents, these your fathers, these;
And not unfitly: for you are so born,
As all your good, or ill's the common-wealth's.
Receive them, you strong guardians; and blest gods,
Make all their actions answer to their bloods:
Let their great titles find increase by them,
Not they by titles. Set them as in place,

So in example, above all the Romans:
And may they know no rivals but themselves.
Let Fortune give them nothing; but attend
Upon their virtue: and that still come forth
Greater than hope, and better than their fame.
Relieve me, fathers, with your general voice.

Senators.
  May all the gods consent to Caesar's wish,
  And add to any honours that may crown
  The hopeful issue of Germanicus

Tib. We thank you, reverend fathers, in their right.

Arr.
  If this were true now! but the space, the space
  Between the breast and lips——Tiberius' heart
  Lies a thought further than another man's.　　[Aside.

Tib.
  My comforts are so flowing in my joys,
  As, in them, all my streams of grief are lost,
  No less than are land-waters in the sea,
  Or showers in rivers; though their cause was such,
  As might have sprinkled ev'n the gods with tears:
  Yet, since the greater doth embrace the less,
  We covetously obey.

Arr. Well acted, Caesar.　　　　　　　[Aside.

Tib.
  And now I am the happy witness made
  Of your so much desired affections
  To this great issue, I could wish, the
  Fates Would here set peaceful period to my days;
  However to my labours, I entreat,
  And beg it of this senate, some fit ease.

Arr. Laugh, fathers, laugh: have you no spleens about you?
　　　　　　　　　　　　[Aside.
Tib.
  The burden is too heavy I sustain
  On my unwilling shoulders; and I pray
  It may be taken off, and reconferred
  Upon the consuls, or some other Roman,
  More able, and more worthy.

Arr. Laugh on still.　　　　　　　[Aside.

Sab. Why this doth render all the rest suspected!

Gal. It poisons all.

Arr. O, do you taste it then?

Sab.
  It takes away my faith to any thing,
  He shall hereafter speak.

Arr.
  Ay, to pray that,
  Which would be to his head as hot as thunder,
  'Gainst which he wears that charm should but the court
  Receive him at his word.

Gal. Hear!

Tib.
  For myself
  I know my weakness, and so little covet,
  Like some gone past, the weight that will oppress me,
  As my ambition is the counter-point.

Arr. Finely maintained; good still!

Sej.
  But Rome, whose blood,
  Whose nerves, whose life, whose very frame relies
  On Caesar's strength, no less than heaven on Atlas,
  Cannot admit it but with general ruin.

Arr. Ah! are you there to bring him off?   [Aside.

Sej.
  Let Caesar
  No more then urge a point so contrary
  To Caesar's greatness, the grieved senate's vows,
  Or Rome's necessity.

Gal. He comes about——

Arr. More nimbly than Vertumnus.

Tib.
  For the publick,
  I may be drawn to shew I can neglect
  All private aims, though I affect my rest;
  But if the senate still command me serve,

I must be glad to practise my obedience.

Arr. You must and will, sir. We do know it.   [Aside.

Senators.
  Caesar,
  Live long and happy, great and royal Caesar;
  The gods preserve thee and thy modesty,
  Thy wisdom and thy innocence

Arr.
  Where is't?
  The prayer is made before the subject.   [Aside.

Senators.
  Guard
  His meekness, Jove; his piety, his care,
  His bounty——

Arr.
  And his subtility, I'll put in:
  Yet he'll keep that himself, without the gods.
  All prayers are vain for him.   [Aside.
Tib.
  We will not hold
  Your patience, fathers, with long answer; but
  Shall still contend to be what you desire,
  And work to satisfy so great a hope.
  Proceed to your affairs.

Arr.
  Now, Silius, guard thee;
  The curtain's drawing. Afer advanceth.   [Aside.

Prae. Silence!

Afer. Cite Caius Silius.

Prae. Caius Silius!

Sil. Here.

Afer.
  The triumph that thou hadst in Germany
  For thy late victory on Sacrovir,
  Thou hast enjoy'd so freely, Caius Silius,
  As no man it envied thee; nor would Caesar,
  Or Rome admit, that thou wert then defrauded
  Of any honours thy deserts could claim,

In the fair service of the common-wealth:
But now, if, after all their loves and graces,
(Thy actions, and their courses being discover'd)
It shall appear to Caesar and this senate,
Thou hast defiled those glories with thy crimes——

Sil. Crimes!

Afer. Patience, Silius.

Sil.
Tell thy mule of patience;
I am a Roman. What are my crimes? proclaim them.
Am I too rich, too honest for the times?
Have I or treasure, jewels, land, or houses
That some informer gapes for? is my strength
Too much to be admitted, or my knowledge?
These now are crimes.

Afer.
  Nay, Silius, if the name
Of crime so touch thee, with what impotence
Wilt thou endure the matter to be search'd?

Sil.
I tell thee, Afer, with more scorn than fear:
Employ your mercenary tongue and art.
Where's my accuser?

Var. Here.

Arr.
Varro, the consul!
Is he thrust in?   [Aside.

Var.
'Tis I accuse thee, Silius.
Against the majesty of Rome, and Caesar,
I do pronounce thee here a guilty cause,
First of beginning and occasioning,
Next, drawing out the war in Gallia,
For which thou late triumph'st; dissembling long
That Sacrovir to be an enemy,
Only to make thy entertainment more.
Whilst thou, and thy wife Sosia, poll'd the province:
Wherein, with sordid, base desire of gain,
Thou hast discredited thy actions' worth,
And been a traitor to the state.

Sil. Thou liest.

Arr. I thank thee, Silius, speak so still and often.

Var.
  If I not prove it, Caesar, but unjustly
  Have call'd him into trial; here I bind
  Myself to suffer, what I claim against him;
  And yield to have what I have spoke, confirm'd
  By judgment of the court, and all good men.

Sil.
  Caesar, I crave to have my cause deferr'd,
  Till this man's consulship be out.

Tib.
  We cannot,
  Nor may we grant it.

Sil.
  Why? shall he design
  My day of trial? Is he my accuser,
  And must he be my judge?

Tib.
  It hath been usual,
  And is a right that custom hath allow'd
  The magistrate, to call forth private men;
  And to appoint their day: which privilege
  We may not in the consul see infringed,
  By whose deep watches, and industrious care
  It is so labour'd, as the common-wealth
  Receive no loss, by any oblique course.

Sil. Caesar, thy fraud is worse than violence.

Tib.
  Silius, mistake us not, we dare not use
  The credit of the consul to thy wrong;
  But only to preserve his place and power,
  So far as it concerns the dignity
  And honour of the state.

Arr. Believe him, Silius.

Cot. Why, so he may, Arruntius.

Arr.
  I say so.

And he may choose too.

Tib.
By the Capitol,
And all our gods, but that the dear republic,
Our sacred laws, and just authority
Are interess'd therein, I should be silent.

Afer.
'Please Caesar to give way unto his trial,
He shall have justice.

Sil.
Nay, I shall have law;
Shall I not, Afer? speak.

Afer. Would you have more?

Sil.
No, my well-spoken man, I would no more;
Nor less: might I enjoy it natural,.
Not taught to speak unto your present ends,
Free from thine, his, and all your unkind handling,
Furious enforcing, most unjust presuming,
Malicious, and manifold applying,
Foul wresting, and impossible construction.

Afer. He raves, he raves.

Sil.
Thou durst not tell me so,
Hadst thou not Crease's warrant.
I can see Whose power condemns me.

Var.
This betrays his spirit:
This doth enough declare him what he is.

Sil. What am I? speak.

Var. An enemy to the state.

Sil.
Because I am an enemy to thee,
And such corrupted ministers o' the state,
That here art made a present instrument
To gratify it with thine own disgrace.

Sej.

This, to the consul, is most insolent,
And impious.

Sil.
Ay, take part. Reveal yourselves,
Alas! I scent not your confederacies,
Your plots, and combinations! I not know
Minion Sejanus hates me: and that all,
This boast of law, and law, is but a form,
A net of Vulcan's filing, a mere ingine,
To take that life by a pretext of justice,
Which you pursue in malice! I want brain,
Or nostril to persuade me, that your ends,
And purposes are made to what they are,
Before my answer! O, you equal gods,
Whose justice not a world of wolf-turn'd men
Shall make me to accuse, howe'er provoked;
Have I for this so oft engaged myself?
Stood in the heat and fervour of a fight,
When Phoebus sooner hath forsook the day
Than I the field, against the blue-eyed Gauls,
And crisped Germans? when our Roman eagles
Have fann'd the fire, with their labouring wings,
And no blow dealt, that left not death behind it?
When I have charged, alone, into the troops
Of curl'd Sicambrians, routed them, and came
Not off, with backward ensigns of a slave;
But forward marks, wounds on my breast and face,
Were meant to thee, O Caesar, and thy Rome?
And have I this return! did I, for this,
Perform so noble and so brave defeat
On Sacrovir! O Jove, let it become me
To boast my deeds, when he whom they concern,
Shall thus forget them.

Afer.
Silius, Silius,
These are the common customs of thy blood,
When it is high with wine, as now with rage:
This well agrees with that intemperate vaunt,
Thou lately mad'st at Agrippina's table,
That, when all other of the troops were prone
To fall into rebellion, only thine
Remain'd in their obedience. Thou wert he
That saved the empire, which had then been lost
Had but thy legions, there, rebell'd, or mutined;
Thy virtue met, and fronted every peril.
Thou gav'st to Caesar, and to Rome their surety;
Their name, their strength, their spirit, and their state,

Their being was a donative from thee.

Arr. Well worded, and most like an orator.

Tib. Is this true, Silius?

Sil.
　Save thy question, Caesar;
　Thy spy of famous credit hath affirm'd it.

Arr. Excellent Roman!

Sab. He doth answer stoutly.

Sej.
　If this be so, there needs no farther cause
　Of crime against him.

Var.
　What can more impeach
　The royal dignity and state of Caesar,
　Than to be urged with a benefit He cannot pay?

Cot.
　In this, all Ceesar's fortune
　Is made unequal to the courtesy.

Lat. His means are clean destroyed that should requite.

Gal. Nothing is great enough for Silius' merit.

Arr. Gallus on that side too! [Aside.

Sil.
　Come, do not hunt,
　And labour so about for circumstance,
　To make him guilty whom you have foredoom'd:
　Take shorter ways, I'll meet your purposes.
　The words were mine, and more I now will say:
　Since I have done thee that great service, Caesar,
　Thou still hast fear'd me; and in place of grace,
　Return'd me hatred: so soon all best turns,
　With doubtful princes, turn deep injuries
　In estimation, when they greater rise
　Than can be answer'd. Benefits, with you,
　Are of no longer pleasure, than you can
　With ease restore them; that transcended once,
　Your studies are not how to thank, but kill.
　It is your nature, to have all men slaves

To you, but you acknowledging to none.
The means that make your greatness, must not come
In mention of it; if it do, it takes
So much away, you think: and that which help'd,
Shall soonest perish, if it stand in eye,
Where it may front, or but upbraid the high.

Got. Suffer him speak no more.

Var. Note but his spirit.

Afer. This shews him in the rest.

Lat. Let him be censured.
Sej. He hath spoke enough to prove him Caesar's foe.

Got. His thoughts look through his words.

Sej. A censure.

Sil.
  Stay,
  Stay, most officious senate, I shall straight
  Delude thy fury. Silius hath not placed
  His guards within him, against fortune's spite,
  So weakly, but he can escape your gripe
  That are but hands of fortune: she herself,
  When virtue doth oppose, must lose her threats!
  All that can happen in humanity,
  The frown of Caesar, proud Sejanus' hatred,
  Base Varro's spleen, and Afer's bloodying tongue,
  The senate's servile flattery, and these
  Muster'd to kill, I'm fortified against;
  And can look down upon: they are beneath me.
  It is not life whereof I stand enamour'd;
  Nor shall my end make me accuse my fate.
  The coward and the valiant man must fall,
  Only the cause and manner how, discerns them:
  Which then are gladdest, when they cost us dearest.
  Romans, if any here be in this senate,
  Would know to mock Tiberius' tyranny,
  Look upon Silius, and so learn to die.   [Stabs himself.

Var. O desperate act!

Arr. An honourable hand!

Tib. Look, is he dead?

Sab. 'Twas nobly struck, and home.

Arr.
  My thought did prompt him to it. Farewell. Silius.
  Be famous ever for thy great example.

Tib.
  We are not pleased in this sad accident,
  That thus hath stalled, and abused our mercy,
  Intended to preserve thee, noble Roman,
  And to prevent thy hopes.

Arr.
  Excellent wolf!
  Now he is full he howls.   [Aside.

Sej.
  Caesar doth wrong
  His dignity and safety thus to mourn
  The deserv'd end of so profest a traitor,
  And doth, by this his lenity, instruct
  Others as factious to the like offence.

Tib.
  The confiscation merely of his state
  Had been enough.

Arr. O, that was gaped for then?   [Aside.

Var. Remove the body.

Sej. Let citation Go out for Sosia.

Gal.
  Let her be proscribed:
  And for the goods, I think it fit that half
  Go to the treasure, half unto the children.

Lep.
  With leave of Caesar, I would think that fourth,
  The which the law doth cast on the informers,
  Should be enough; the rest go to the children.
  Wherein the prince shall shew humanity,
  And bounty; not to force them by their want,
  Which in their parents' trespass they deserv'd,
  To take ill courses.

Tib. It shall please us.

Arr.
   Ay,
   Out of necessity. This Lepidus
   Is grave and honest, and I have observed
   A moderation still in all his censures.

Sab.
   And bending to the better——Stay, who's this?

   Enter SATRIUS and NATTA, with CREMUTIUS CORDUS guarded.

   Cremutius Cordus! What! is he brought in?

Arr.
   More blood into the banquet! Noble Cordus,
   I wish thee good: be as thy writings, free,
   And honest.

Tib. What is he?

Sej. For the Annals, Caesar.

Prae. Cremutius Cordus!

Cor. Here.

Prae.
   Satrius Secundus,
   Pinnarius Natta, you are his accusers.

Arr.
   Two of Sejanus' blood-hounds, whom he breeds
   With human flesh, to bay at citizens.

Afer. Stand forth before the senate, and confront him.

Sat.
   I do accuse thee here, Cremutius Cordus,
   To be a man factious and dangerous,
   A sower of sedition in the state,
   A turbulent and discontented spirit,
   Which I will prove from thine own writings, here,
   The Annals thou hast publish'd; where thou bit'st
   The present age, and with a viper's tooth,
   Being a member of it, dar'st that ill
   Which never yet degenerous bastard did
   Upon his parent.

Nat.
    To this, I subscribe;
    And, forth a world of more particulars,
    Instance in only one: comparing men,
    And times, thou praisest Brutus, and affirm'st
    That Cassius was the last of all the Romans.

Cot. How! what are we then?

Var. What is Caesar? nothing?

Afer.
    My lords, this strikes at every Roman's private,
    In whom reigns gentry, and estate of spirit,
    To have a Brutus brought in parallel,
    A parricide, an enemy of his country,
    Rank'd, and preferr'd to any real worth
    That Rome now holds. This is most strangely invective,
    Most full of spite, and insolent upbraiding.
    Nor is't the time alone is here disprised,
    But the whole man of time, yea, Caesar's self
    Brought in disvalue; and he aimed at most,
    By oblique glance of his licentious pen.
    Caesar, if Cassius were the last of Romans,
    Thou hast no name.

Tib. Let's hear him answer. Silence!

Cor.
    So innocent I am of fact, my lords,
    As but my words are argued: yet those words
    Not reaching either prince or prince's parent:
    The which your law of treason comprehends.
    Brutus and Cassius I am charged to have praised;
    Whose deeds, when many more, besides myself,
    Have writ, not one hath mention'd without honour.
    Great Titus Livius, great for eloquence,
    And faith amongst us, in his history,
    With so great praises Pompey did extol,
    As oft Augustus call'd him a Pompeian:
    Yet this not hurt their friendship. In his book
    He often names Scipio, Afranius,
    Yea, the same Cassius, and this Brutus too,
    As worthiest men; not thieves and parricides,
    Which notes upon their fames are now imposed.
    Asinius Pollio's writings quite throughout
    Give them a noble memory; so Messala
    Renown'd his general Cassius: yet both these
    Lived with Augustus, full of wealth and honours,

  To Cicero's book, where Cato was heav'd up
Equal with Heaven, what else did Caesar answer,
Being then dictator, but with a penn'd oration,
As if before the judges? Do but see
Antonius' letters; read but Brutus' pleadings:
What vile reproach they hold against Augustus,
False, I confess, but with much bitterness.
The epigrams of Bibaculus and Catullus
Are read, full stuft with spite of both the Caesars;
Yet deified Julius, and no less Augustus,
Both bore them, and contemn'd them: I not know,
Promptly to speak it, whether done with more
Temper, or wisdom; for such obloquies
If they despised be, they die supprest;
But if with rage acknowledg'd, they are confest.
The Greeks I slip, whose license not alone,
But also lust did scape unpunished:
Or where some one, by chance, exception took,
He words with words revenged. But, in my work,
What could be aim'd more free, or farther off
From the time's scandal, than to write of those,
Whom death from grace or hatred had exempted?
Did I, with Brutus and with Cassius,
Arm'd, and possess'd of the Philippi fields,
Incense the people in the civil cause,
With dangerous speeches? Or do they, being slain
Seventy years since, as by their images,
Which not the conqueror hath defaced, appears,
Retain that guilty memory with writers?
Posterity pays every man his honour;
Nor shall there want, though I condemned am,
That will not only Cassius well approve,
And of great Brutus' honour mindful be,
But that will also mention make of me.

Arr. Freely and nobly spoken!

Sab.
 With good temper;
 I like him, that he is not moved with passion.

Arr. He puts them to their whisper.

Tib.
 Take him hence;
 We shall determine of him at next sitting.
       [*Exeunt Officers with Cordus.*
Cot.
 Mean time, give order, that his books be burnt,

To the aediles.

Sej. You have well advised.

Afer.
It fits not such licentious things should live
T'upbraid the age.

Arr. If the age were good, they might.

Lat. Let them be burnt.

Gal. All sought, and burnt to-day.

Prae. The court is up; lictors, resume the fasces.
          [Exeunt all but Arruntius, Sabinus, and Lepidus.
Arr.
Let them be burnt! O, how ridiculous
Appears the senate's brainless diligence,
Who think they can, with present power, extinguish
The memory of all succeeding times!

Sab.
'Tis true; when, contrary, the punishment
Of wit, doth make the authority increase.
Nor do they aught, that use this cruelty
Of interdiction, and this rage of burning,
But purchase to themselves rebuke and shame,
And to the writers an eternal name.

Lep.
It is an argument the times are sore,
When virtue cannot safely be advanced;
Nor vice reproved.

Arr.
Ay, noble Lepidus;
Augustus well foresaw what we should suffer
Under Tiberius, when he did pronounce
The Roman race most wretched, that should live
Between so slow jaws, and so long a bruising.   [Exeunt.
      SCENE II.——A Room in the Palace.
        Enter TIBERIUS and SEJANUS.

Tib.
This business hath succeeded well, Sejanus,
And quite removed all jealousy of practice
'Gainst Agrippina, and our nephews. Now,
We must bethink us how to plant our ingine,

For th' other pair, Sabinus and Arruntius,
And Gallus too: howe'er he flatter us,
His heart we know.

Sej.
Give it some respite, Caesar.
Time shall mature, and bring to perfect crown,
What we, with so good vultures have begun:
Sabinus shall be next.

Tib. Rather Arruntius.

Sej.
By any means, preserve him. His frank tongue
Being let the reins, would take away all thought
Of malice, in your course against the rest:
We must keep him to stalk with.

Tib.
Dearest head,
To thy most fortunate design I yield it.

Sej.
Sir,——I have been so long train'd up in grace,
First with your father, great Augustus; since,
With your most happy bounties so familiar
As I not sooner would commit my hopes
Or wishes to the gods. than to your ears.
Nor have I ever, yet, been covetous
Of over-bright and dazzling honour; rather
To watch and travail in great Caesar's safety,
With the most common soldier.

Tib. 'Tis confest.

Sej.
The only gain, and which I count most fair
Of all my fortunes, is, that mighty Caesar
Has thought me worthy his alliance. Hence
Begin my hopes.

Tib. Umph!

Sej.
I have heard, Augustus,
In the bestowing of his daughter, thought
But even of gentlemen of Rome: if so,——
I know not how to hope so great a favour——
But if a husband should be sought for Livia,

And I he had in mind, as Caesar's friend,
I would but use the glory of the kindred:
It should not make me slothful, or less caring
For Caesar's state: it were enough to me
It did confirm, and strengthen my weak house,
Against the now unequal opposition
Of Agrippina; and for dear regard
Unto my children, this I wish: myself
Have no ambition farther than to end
My days in service of so dear a master.

Tib.
We cannot but commend thy piety,
Most loved Sejanus, in acknowledging
Those bounties; which we, faintly, such remember——
But to thy suit. The rest of mortal men,
In all their drifts and counsels, pursue profit;
Princes alone are of a different sort,
Directing their main actions still to fame:
We therefore will take time to think and answer.
For Livia she can best, herself, resolve
If she will marry, after Drusus, or
Continue in the family; besides,
She hath a mother, and a grandam yet,
Whose nearer counsels she may guide her by:
But I will simply deal. That enmity
Thou fear'st in Agrippina, would burn more,
If Livia's marriage should, as 'twere in parts,
Divide the imperial house; an emulation
Between the women might break forth; and discord
Ruin the sons and nephews on both hands.
What if it cause some present difference?
Thou art not safe, Sejanus, if thou prove it.
Canst thou believe, that Livia, first the wife
To Caius Caesar, then my Drusus, now
Will be contented to grow old with thee,
Born but a private gentleman of Rome,
And raise thee with her loss, if not her shame?
Or say that I should wish it, canst thou think
The senate, or the people (who have seen
Her brother, father, and our ancestors,
In highest place of empire) will endure it!
The state thou hold'st already, is in talk;
Men murmur at thy greatness; and the noble!
Stick not, in public, to upbraid thy climbing
Above our father's favours, or thy scale:
And dare accuse me, from their hate to thee.
Be wise, dear friend. We would not hide these things,
For friendship's dear respect: Nor will we stand

    Adverse to thine, or Livia's designments.
    What we have purposed to thee, in our thought,
    And with what near degrees of love to bind thee,
    And make thee equal to us; for the present,
    We will forbear to speak. Only thus much
    Believe, our loved Sejanus, we not know
    That height in blood or honour, which thy virtue
    And mind to us, may not aspire with merit.
    And this we'll publish on all watch'd occasion
    The senate or the people shall present.

Sej.
    I am restored, and to my sense again,
    Which I had lost in this so blinding suit.
    Caesar hath taught me better to refuse,
    Than I knew how to ask. How pleaseth Caesar
    T' embrace my late advice for leaving Rome!

Tib. We are resolved.

Sej.
    Here are some motives more,   [Gives him a paper
    Which I have thought on since, may more confirm.

Tib.
    Careful Sejanus! we will straight peruse them:
    Go forward in our main design, and prosper.   [Exit.

Sej.
    If those but take, I shall. Dull, heavy Caesar!
    Wouldst thou tell me, thy favours were made crimes,
    And that my fortunes were esteem'd thy faults,
    That thou for me wert hated, and not think
    I would with winged haste prevent that change,
    When thou might'st win all to thyself again,
    By forfeiture of me! Did those fond words
    Fly swifter from thy lips, than this my brain,
    This sparkling forge, created me an armour
    T' encounter chance and thee? Well, read my charms,
    And may they lay that hold upon thy senses,
    As thou hadst snuft up hemlock, or ta'en down
    The juice of poppy and of mandrakes. Sleep,
    Voluptuous Caesar, and security
    Seize on 'thy stupid powers, and leave them dead
    To public cares; awake but to thy lusts,
    The strength of which makes thy libidinous soul
    Itch to leave Rome! and I have thrust it on;
    With blaming of the city business,
    The multitude of suits, the confluence

Of suitors; then their importunacies,
The manifold distractions he must suffer,
Besides ill-rumours, envies, and reproaches,
All which a quiet and retired life,
Larded with ease and pleasure, did avoid:
And yet for any weighty and great affair,
The fittest place to give the soundest counsels.
By this I shall remove him both from thought
And knowledge of his own most dear affairs;
Draw all dispatches through my private hands;
Know his designments, and pursue mine own;
Make mine own strengths by giving suits and places.
Conferring dignities and offices;
And these that hate me now, wanting access
To him, will make their envy none, or less:
For when they see me arbiter of all,
They must observe; or else, with Caesar fall. [Exit

SCENE III.—Another Room in the same.
Enter TIBEBIUS.

Tib.
To marry Livia! will no less, Sejanus,
Content thy aim? no lower object? well!
Thou know'st how thou art wrought into our trust;
Woven in our design; and think'st we must
Now use thee, whatsoe'er thy projects are:
'Tis true. But yet with caution and fit care.
And, now we better think——who's there within?

Enter an Officer.

Off. Caesar!

Tib.
To leave our journey off, were sin
'Gainst our decreed delights; and would appear
Doubt; or, what less becomes a prince, low fear.
Yet doubt hath law, and fears have their excuse.
Where princes' states plead necessary use;
As ours doth now: more in Sejanus' pride,
Than all fell Agrippina's hates beside.
Those are the dreadful enemies we raise
With favours, and make dangerous with praise;
The injured by us may have will alike,
But 'tis the favourite hath the power to strike;
And fury ever boils more high and strong,
Heat with ambition, than revenge of wrong.
'Tis then a part of supreme skill, to grace
No man too much; but hold a certain space
Between the ascender's rise, and thine own flat,
Lest, when all rounds be reach'd, his aim be that.

    'Tis thought.   [Aside.]
    Is Macro in the palace? see:
    If not, go seek him, to come to us.——   [Exit Offi.]
    He must be the organ we must work by now;
    Though none less apt for trust: need doth allow
    What choice would not. I have heard that aconite,
    Being timely taken, hath a healing might
    Against the scorpion's stroke: the proof we'll give:
    That, while two poisons wrestle, we may live.
    He hath a spirit too working to be used
    But to the encounter of his like; excused
    Are wiser sov'reigns then, that raise one ill
    Against another, and both safely kill:
    The prince that feeds great natures, they will slay him;
    Who nourisheth a lion must obey him.——
                    Be-enter Officer, with MACRO.
    Macro, we sent for you.

Mac. I heard so, Caesar.

Tib.
    Leave us awhile.——   [Exit Officer.]
    When you shall know. good Macro,
    The causes of our sending, and the ends,
    You will then hearken nearer; and be pleas'd
    You stand so high both in our choice and trust.

Mac.
    The humblest place in Caesar's choice or trust,
    May make glad Macro proud; without ambition.
    Save to do Caesar service.

Tib.
    Leave your courtings.
    We are in purpose, Macro, to depart
    The city for a time, and see Campania;
    Not for our pleasures, but to dedicate
    A pair of temples, one to Jupiter
    At Capua; th' other at Nola, to Augustus:
    In which great work, perhaps our stay will be
    Beyond our will produced...Now since we are
    Not ignorant what danger may be born
    Out of our shortest absence in a state
    So subject unto envy, and embroil'd
    With hate and faction; we have thought on thee,
    Amongst a field of Romans, worthiest Macro,
    To be our eye and ear: to keep strict watch
    On Agrippina, Nero, Drusus; ay,
    And on Sejanus: not that we distrust

His loyalty, or do repent one grace
Of all that heap we have conferred on him;
For that were to disparage our election,
And call that judgment now in doubt, which then
Seem'd as unquestion'd as an oracle-
But, greatness hath his cankers. Worms and moths
Breed out of too much humour, in the things
Which after they consume, transferring quite
The substance of their makers into themselves.
Macro is sharp, and apprehends: besides,
I know him subtle, close, wise, and well-read
In man, and his large nature; he hath studied
Affections, passions, knows their springs, their ends,
Which way, and whether they will work: 'tis proof
Enough of his great merit, that we trust him.
Then to a point, because our conference
Cannot be long without suspicion——
Here, Macro, we assign thee, both to spy,
Inform, and chastise; think, and use thy means,
Thy ministers, what, where, on whom thou wilt;
Explore, plot, practise: all thou dost in this
Shall be, as if the Senate, or the laws
Had given it privilege, and thou thence styled
The saviour both of Caesar and of Rome.
We will not take thy answer but in act:
Whereto, as thou proceed'st, we hope to hear
By trusted messengers. If't be inquired,
Wherefore we call'd you, say you have in charge
To see our chariots ready, and our horse.——
Be still our loved and, shortly, honour'd Macro.

Mac.
   I will not ask, why Caesar bids do this;
But joy that he bids me. It is the bliss
Of courts to be employ'd, no matter how;
A prince's power makes all his actions virtue.
We, whom he works by, are dumb instruments,
To do, but not inquire: his great intents
Are to be served, not search'd. Yet, as that bow
Is most in hand, whose owner best doth know
To affect his aims; so let that statesman hope
Most use, most price, can hit his prince's scope.
Nor must he look at what, or whom to strike,
But loose at all; each mark must be alike.
Were it to plot against the fame, the life
Of one, with whom I twinn'd; remove a wife
From my warm side, as loved as is the air;
Practise sway each parent; draw mine heir
In compass, though but one; work all my kin

To swift perdition; leave no untrain'd engine,
For friendship, or for innocence; nay, make
The gods all guilty; I would undertake
This, being imposed me, both with gain and ease:
The way to rise is to obey and please.
He that will thrive in state, he must neglect
The trodden paths that truth and right respect;
And prove new, wilder ways: for virtue there
Is not that narrow thing, she is elsewhere;
Men's fortune there is virtue; reason their will;
Their license, law; and their observance, skill.
Occasion is their foil; conscience, their stain;
Profit their lustre; and what else is, vain.
If then it be the lust of Caesar's power,
To have raised Sejanus up, and in an hour
O'erturn him, tumbling down, from height of all;
We are his ready engine: and his fall
May be our rise. It is no uncouth thing
To see fresh buildings from old ruins spring.   [Exit.

ACT IV

SCENE I.-An Apartment in AGRIPPINA'S House.
Enter GALLUS and AGRIPPINA.

Gal. You must have patience, royal Agrippina.

Agr.
   I must have vengeance, first; and that were nectar
Unto my famish'd spirits. O, my fortune,
Let it be sudden thou prepar'st against me;
Strike all my powers of understanding blind.
And ignorant of destiny to come!
Let me not fear that cannot hope.

Gal.
   Dear princess,
These tyrannies on yourself, are worse than Caesar's.

Agr.
   Is this the happiness of being born great?
Still to be aim'd at? still to be suspected?
To live the subject of all jealousies?
At least the colour made, if not the ground
To every painted danger? who would not
Choose once to fall, than thus to hang for ever?

Gal. You might be safe if you would——

Agr.
   What, my Gallus!
Be lewd Sejanus' strumpet, or the bawd
To Caesar's lusts, he now is gone to practise?
Not these are safe, where nothing is. Yourself,
While thus you stand but by me, are not safe.
Was Silius safe? or the good Sosia safe?
Or was my niece, dear Claudia Pulchra, safe,
Or innocent Furnius? they that latest have
(By being made guilty) added reputation
To Afer's eloquence? O, foolish friends,
Could not so fresh example warn your loves,
But you must buy my favours with that loss
Unto yourselves; and when you might perceive
That Caesar's cause of raging must forsake him,
Before his will! Away, good Gallus, leave me.
Here to be seen, is danger; to speak, treason:
To do me least observance, is call'd faction.
You are unhappy in me, and I in all.

    Where are my sons, Nero and Drusus?   We
Are they be shot at; let us fall apart;
Not in our ruins, sepulchre our friends.
Or shall we do some action like offence,
To mock their studies that would make us faulty,
And frustrate practice by preventing it?
The danger's like: for what they can contrive,
They will make good. No innocence is safe,
When power contests: nor can they trespass more,
Whose only being was all crime before.

                    Enter NERO, DRUSUS, and CALIGULA.

Ner. You hear Sejanus is come back from Caesar?

Gal. No. How? disgraced?

Dru. More graced now than ever.

Cal. By what mischance?

Cal.
  A fortune like enough
  Once to be bad.

Dru. But turn'd too good to both.

Gal. What was't?

Ner.
  Tiberius sitting at his meat,
  In a farm-house they call Spelunca, sited
  By the sea-side, among the Fundane hills,
  Within a natural cave; part of the grot,
  About the entry, fen, and overwhelm'd
  Some of the waiters; others ran away:
  Only Sejanus with his knees, hands, face,
  O'erhanging Caesar, did oppose himself
  To the remaining ruins, and was found
  In that so labouring posture by the soldiers
  That came to succour him. With which adventure,
  He hath so fix'd himself in Caesar's trust,
  As thunder cannot move him, and is come
  With all the height of Caesar's praise to Rome.

Agr.
  And power, to turn those ruins all on us;
  And bury whole posterities beneath them.
  Nero, and Drusus, and Caligula,

Your places are the next, and therefore most
In their offence. Think on your birth and blood.
Awake your spirits, meet their violence;
'Tis princely when a tyrant doth oppose,
And is a fortune sent to exercise
Your virtue, as the wind doth try strong trees,
Who by vexation grow more sound and firm.
After your father's fall, and uncle's fate,
What can you hope, but all the change of stroke
That force or sleight can give? then stand upright;
And though you do not act, yet suffer nobly:
Be worthy of my womb, and take strong chear;
What we do know will come, we should not fear. [Exeunt.

SCENE ll.——The Street

Enter MACRO.

Mac.
Return'd so soon! renew'd in trust and grace!
Is Caesar then so weak, or hath the place
But wrought this alteration with the air;
And he, on next remove, will all repair?
Macro, thou art engaged: and what before
Was public; now, must be thy private, more.
The weal of Caesar, fitness did imply;
But thine own fate confers necessity
On thy employment; and the thoughts born nearest
Unto ourselves, move swiftest still, and dearest.
If he recover, thou art lost; yea, all
The weight of preparation to his fall
Will turn on thee, and crush thee: therefore strike
Before he settle, to prevent the like
Upon thyself. He doth his vantage know,
That makes it home, and gives the foremost blow. [Exit.

SCENE Ill.-An upper Room of AGRIPPINA'S HOUSE.

Enter LATIARIS, RUFUS, and OPSIUS

Lat.
It is a service lord Sejanus will
See well requited, and accept of nobly.
Here place yourself between the roof and ceiling;
And when I bring him to his words of danger,
Reveal yourselves, and take him.

Ruf. Is he come?

Lat. I'll now go fetch him.

Ops.
  With good speed.-I long
  To merit from the state in such an action.

Ruf.
  I hope, it will obtain the consulship
  For one of us...

Ops.
  We cannot think of less,
  To bring in one so dangerous as Sabinus.

Ruf.
  He was follower of Germanicus,
  And still is an observer of his wife
  And children, though they be declined in grace
  A daily visitant, keeps them company
  In private and in public, and is noted
  To be the only client of the house:
  Pray Jove. he will be free to Latiaris.

Ops.
  He's allied to him, and doth trust him well.
  Ruf: And he'll requite his trust!

Ops.
  To do an office
  So grateful to the state, I know no man
  But would strain nearer bands, than kindred——

Ruf.
  List!
  I hear them come.

Ops. Shift to our holes with silence.   [They retire

          Re-enter LATIARIS and SABINUS.

Lat.
  It is a noble constancy you shew
  To this afflicted house; that not like others,
  The friends of season, you do follow fortune,
  And, in the winter of their fate, forsake
  The place whose glories warm'd you. You are just,
  And worthy such a princely patron's love,
  As was the world's renown'd Germanicus:
  Whose ample merit when I call to thought,
  And see his wife and issue, objects made
  To so much envy, jealousy, and hate;
  It makes me ready to accuse the gods

  Of negligence, as men of tyranny.

Sab. They must be patient, so must we.

Lat.
 O Jove,
 What will become of us or of the times,
 When, to be high or noble, are made crimes,
 When land and treasure are most dangerous faults!

Sab.
 Nay, when our table, yea our bed, assaults
 Our peace and safety? when our writings are,
 By any envious instruments, that dare
 Apply them to the guilty, made to speak
 What they will have to fit their tyrannous wreak?
 When ignorance is scarcely innocence;
 And knowledge made a capital offence!
 When not so much, but the bare empty shade
 Of liberty is raft us; and we made
 The prey to greedy vultures and vile spies,
 That first transfix us with their murdering eyes.

Lat.
 Methinks the genius of the Roman race
 Should not be so extinct, but that bright flame
 Of liberty might be revived again,
 (Which no good man but. with his life should lose)
 And we not sit like spent and patient fools,
 Still puffing in the dark at one poor coal,
 Held on by hope till the last spark is out.
 The cause is public, and the honour, name,
 The immortality of every soul,
 That is not bastard or a slave in Rome,
 Therein concern'd: whereto, if men would change
 The wearied arm, and for the weighty shield
 So long sustain'd, employ the facile sword,
 We might soon have assurance of our vows.
 This ass's fortitude doth tire us all:
 It must be active valour must redeem
 Our loss, or none. The rock and 'our hard steel
 Should meet to enforce those glorious fires again,
 Whose splendour cheer'd the world, and heat gave life,
 No less than doth the sun's. Sab. 'Twere better stay
 In lasting darkness, and despair of day.
 No ill should force the subject undertake
 Against the sovereign, more than hell should make
 The gods do wrong. A good man should and must
 Sit rather down with loss, than rise unjust.

> Though, when the Romans first did yield themselves
> To one man's power, they did not mean their lives,
> Their fortunes and their liberties, should be
> His absolute spoil, as purchased by the sword.

Lat.
> Why we are worse, if to be slaves, and bond
> To Caesar's slave be such, the proud Sejanus!
> He that is all, does all, gives Caesar leave
> To hide his ulcerous and anointed face,
> With his bald crown at Rhodes, while he here stalks
> Upon the heads of Romans, and their princes,
> Familiarly to empire.

Sab.
> Now you touch
> A point indeed, wherein he shews his art,
> As well as power.

Lat.
> And villainy in both.
> Do you observe where Livia lodges? how
> Drusus came dead? what men have been cut off?

Sab.
> Yes, those are things removed: I nearer look'd
> Into his later practice, where he stands
> Declared a master in his mystery.
> First, ere Tiberius went, he wrought his fear
> To think that Agrippina sought his death.
> Then put those doubts in her; sent her oft word.
> Under the show of friendship, to beware
> Of Caesar, for he laid to poison her:
> Drave them to frowns, to mutual jealousies,
> Which, now, in visible hatred are burst out.
> Since, he hath had his hired instruments
> To work on Nero, and to heave him up;
> To tell him Caesar's old, that all the people,
> Yea, all the army have their eyes on him;
> That both do long to have him undertake
> Something of worth, to give the world a hope;
> Bids him to court their grace: the easy youth
> Perhaps gives ear, which straight he writes to Caesar;
> And with this comment: See yon dangerous boy;
> Note but the practice of the mother, there;
> She's tying him for purposes at hand,
> With men of sword. Here's Caesar put in fright
> 'Gainst son and mother. Yet, he leaves not thus.
> The second brother, Drusus, a fierce nature,

And fitter for his snares, because ambitious
And full of envy, him he clasps and hugs,
Poisons with praise, tells him what hearts he wears,
How bright he stands in popular expectance;
That Rome doth suffer with him in the wrong
His mother does him, by preferring Nero:
Thus sets he them asunder, each 'gainst other,
Projects the course that serves him to condemn,
Keeps in opinion of a friend to all,
And all drives on to ruin.

Lat. Caesar sleeps, And nods at this.

Sab.
 Would he might ever sleep,
 Bogg'd in his filthy lusts!   [Opsius and Rufus rush in.

Ops. Treason to Caesar!

Ruf.
 Lay hands upon the traitor, Latiaris,
 Or take the name thyself.

Lat. I am for Caesar.

Sab. Am I then catch'd?

Ruf. How think you, sir? you are.

Sab.
 Spies of this head, so white, so full of years!
 Well, my most reverend monsters, you may live
 To see yourselves thus snared.

Ops, Away with him!

Lat. Hale him away.

Ruf.
 To be a spy for traitors,
 Is honourable vigilance.

Sab.
 You do well,
 My most officious instruments of state;
 Men of all uses: drag me hence, away.
 The year is well begun, and I fall fit
 To be an offering to Sejanus. Go!

Ops. Cover him with his garments, hide his face.

Sab.
It shall not need. Forbear your rude assault.
The fault's not shameful, villainy makes a fault. [Exeunt.
SCENE IV.——The Street before AGRIPPINA.'S House.

Enter MACRO and CALIGULA.

Mac.
Sir, but observe how thick your dangers meet
In his clear drifts! your mother and your brothers,
Now cited to the senate; their friend Gallus,
Feasted to-day by Caesar, since committed!
Sabinus here we met, hurried to fetters:
The senators all strook with fear and silence,
Save those whose hopes depend not on good means,
But force their private prey from public spoil.
And you must know, if here you stay, your state
Is sure to be the subject of his hate, As now the object.

Gal. What would you advise me?

Mac.
To go for Capreae presently; and there
Give up yourself entirely to your uncle.
Tell Caesar (since your mother is accused
To fly for succours to Augustus' statue,
And to the army with your brethren) you
Have rather chose to place your aids in him,
Than live suspected; or in hourly fear
To be thrust out, by bold Sejanus' plots:
Which, you shall confidently urge to be
Most full of peril to the state, and Caesar,
As being laid to his peculiar ends,
And not to be let run with common safety.
All which, upon the second, I'll make plain,
So both shall love and trust with Caesar gain.

Gal. Away then, let's prepare us for our journey. [Exeunt
SCENE V.-Another part of the Street.

Enter ARRUNTIUS.

Arr.
Still dost thou suffer, heaven! will no flame,
No heat of sin, make thy just wrath to boil
In thy distemper'd bosom, and o'erflow
The pitchy blazes of impiety,

    Kindled beneath thy throne! Still canst thou sleep,
Patient, while vice doth make an antick face
At thy dread power, and blow dust and smoke
Into thy nostrils! Jove! will nothing wake thee?
Must vile Sejanus pull thee by the beard,
Ere thou wilt open thy black-lidded eye,
And look him dead? Well! snore on, dreaming gods,
And let this last of that proud giant-race
Heave mountain upon mountain, 'gainst your state——
Be good unto me, Fortune and you powers,
Whom I, expostulating, have profaned;
I see what's equal with a prodigy,
A great, a noble Roman, and an honest,
Live an old man!——
                    Enter LEPIDUS.
          O Marcus Lepidus,
When is our turn to bleed? Thyself and I,
Without our boast, are almost all the few
Left to be honest in these impious times.

Lep.
    What we are left to be, we will be, Lucius;
Though tyranny did stare as wide as death,
To fright us from it.

Arr. 'T hath so on Sabinus.

Lep.
    I saw him now drawn from the Gemonies,
And, what increased the direness of the fact,
His faithful dog, upbraiding all us Romans,
Never forsook the corps, but, seeing it thrown
Into the stream, leap'd in, and drown'd with it.

Arr.
    O act, to be envied him of us men!
We are the next the hook lays hold on, Marcus:
What are thy arts, good patriot, teach them me,
That have preserved thy hairs to this white dye,
And kept so reverend and so dear a head
Safe on his comely shoulders?

Lep.
    Arts, Arruntius!
None, but the plain and passive fortitude,
To suffer and be silent; never stretch
These arms against the torrent; live at home,
With my own thoughts, and innocence about me,
Not tempting the wolves' jaws: these are my arts.

Arr.
  I would begin to study 'em, if I thought
  They would secure me. May I pray to Jove
  In secret and be safe? ay, or aloud,
  With open wishes, so I do not mention
  Tiberius or Sejanus? yes, I must,
  If I speak out. 'Tis hard that. May I think,
  And not be rack'd? What danger is't to dream,
  Talk in one's sleep, or cough? Who knows the law?
  May I shake my head without a comment? say
  It rains, or it holds up, and not be thrown
  Upon the Gemonies? These now are things,
  Whereon men's fortune, yea, their faith depends.
  Nothing hath privilege 'gainst the violent ear.
  No place, no day, no hour, we see, is free,
  Not our religious and most sacred times,
  From some one kind of cruelty: all matter
  Nay, all occasion pleaseth. Madmen's rage,
  The idleness of drunkards, women's nothing,
  Jester's simplicity, all, all is good
  That can be catcht at...Nor is now the event
  Of any person, or for any crime,
  To be expected; for 'tis always one:
  Death, with some little difference of place,
  Or time——What's this? Prince Nero, guarded!
              Enter LACO and NERO, with Guards.
Lac.
  On, lictors, keep your way. My lords, forbear.
  On pain of Caesar's wrath, no man attempt
  Speech with the prisoner.

Nero.
  Noble friends, be safe;
  To lose yourselves for words, were as vain hazard,
  As unto me small comfort: fare you well.
  Would all Rome's sufferings in my fate did dwell!

Lac. Lictors, away.

Lep. Where goes he, Laco?

Lac.
  Sir,
  He's banish'd into Pontia by the senate.

Arr.
  Do I see, hear, and feel? May I trust sense,
  Or doth my phant'sie form it?

Lep. Where's his brother?

Lac. Drusus is prisoner in the palace.

Arr. Ha!
  I smell it now: 'tis rank. Where's Agrippina?

Lac. The princess is confined to Pandataria.

Arr.
  Bolts, Vulcan; bolts for Jove! Phoebus, thy bow;
  Stern Mars, thy sword: and, blue-ey'd maid, thy spear;
  Thy club, Alcides: all the armoury
  Of heaven is too little!——Ha!——to guard
  The gods, I meant. Fine, rare dispatch I this same
  Was swiftly born! Confined, imprison'd, banish'd?
  Most tripartite! the cause, sir?

Lac. Treason.

Arr.
  O!
  The complement of all accusings! that
  Will hit, when all else fails.

Lep.
  This turn is strange!
  But yesterday the people would not hear,
  Far less objected, but cried Caesar's letters
  Were false and forged; that all these plots were malice;
  And that the ruin of the prince's house
  Was practised' gainst his knowledge. Where are now
  Their voices, now, that they behold his heirs
  Lock'd up, disgraced, led into exile?

Arr.
  Hush'd,
  Drown'd in their bellies. Wild Sejanus' breath
  Hath, like a whirlwind, scatter'd that poor dust,
  With this rude blast——We'll talk no treason, sir,
          [Turns to Laco and the rest
  If that be it you stand for. Fare you well.
  We have no need of horse-leeches. Good spy,
  Now you are spied, be gone.
          [Exeunt Laco, Nero, and Guards.
Lep.
  I fear you wrong him:
  He has the voice to be an honest Roman.

Arr.
    And trusted to this office! Lepidus,
    I'd sooner trust Greek Sinon, than a man
    Our state employs. He's gone: and being gone,
    I dare tell you, whom I dare better trust,
    That our night-eyed Tiberius doth not see
    His minion's drifts; or, if he do, he's not
    So arrant subtile, as we fools do take him;
    To breed a mungrel up, in his own house,
    With his own blood, and, if the good gods please,
    At his own throat, flesh him, to take a leap.
    I do not beg it, heaven; but if the fates
    Grant it these eyes, they must not wink.

Lep.
    They must
    Not see it, Lucius.

Arr. Who should let them?

Lep.
    Zeal,
    And duty: with the thought he is our prince.

Arr.
    He is our monster: forfeited to vice
    So far, as no rack'd virtue can redeem him.
    His loathed person fouler than all crimes:
    An emperor, only in his lusts. Retired,
    From all regard of his own fame, or Rome's,
    Into an obscure island; where he lives
    Acting his tragedies with a comic face,
    Amidst his route of Chaldees: spending hours,
    Days, weeks, and months, in the unkind abuse
    Of grave astrology, to the bane of men,
    Casting the scope of men's nativities,
    And having found aught worthy in their fortune,
    Kill, or precipitate them in the sea,
    And boast, he can mock fate. Nay, muse not: these
    Are far from ends of evil, scarce degrees.
    He hath his slaughter-house at Capreae;
    Where he doth study murder, as an art;
    And they are dearest in his grace, that can
    Devise the deepest tortures. Thither, too,
    He hath his boys, and beauteous girls ta'en up
    Out of our noblest houses, the best form'd,
    Best nurtured, and most modest; what's their good,
    Serves to provoke his bad. Some are allured,
    Some threaten'd; others, by their friends detained,

   Are ravish'd hence, like captives, and, in sight
   Of their most grieved parents, dealt away
   Unto his spintries, sellaries, and slaves,
   Masters of strange and new commented lusts,
   For which wise nature hath not left a name.
   To this (what most strikes us, and bleeding Rome)
   He is, with all his craft, become the ward
   To his own vassal, a stale catamite:
   Whom he, upon our low and suffering necks,
   Hath raised from excrement to side the gods,
   And have his proper sacrifice in Rome:
   Which Jove beholds, and yet will sooner rive
   A senseless oak with thunder than his trunk!——

          Re-enter LACO with POMPONIUS and MINUTIUS.

Lac.
   These letters make men doubtful what t' expect,
   Whether his coming, or his death.

Pom.
   Troth, both:
   And which comes soonest, thank the gods for.

Arr.
   List!
   Their talk is Caesar; I would hear all voices.

          [Arrunt. and Lepidus stand aside

Min.
   One day, he's well; and will return to Rome;
   The next day, sick; and knows not when to hope it.

Lac.
   True; and to-day, one of Sejanus' friends
   Honour'd by special writ; and on the morrow
   Another punish'd——

Pom. By more special writ.

Min.
   This man receives his praises of Sejanus,
   A second but slight mention, a third none,
   A fourth rebukes: and thus he leaves the senate
   Divided and suspended, all uncertain.

Lac.
   These forked tricks, I understand them not:
   Would he would tell us whom he loves or hates,
   That we might follow, without fear or doubt.

Arr.
  Good Heliotrope! Is this your honest man?
  Let him be yours so still; he is my knave.

Pom.
  I cannot tell, Sejanus still goes on,
  And mounts, we see; new statues are advanced,
  Fresh leaves of titles, large inscriptions read,
  His fortune sworn by, himself new gone out
  Caesar's colleague in the fifth consulship;
  More altars smoke to him than all the gods:
  What would we more?

Arr.
  That the dear smoke would choke him,
  That would I more.
Lep. Peace, good Arruntius.

Lat.
  But there are letters come, they say, ev'n now,
  Which do forbid that last.

Min. Do you hear so?

Lac. Yes.

Pom. By Castor, that's the worst.

Arr. By Pollux, best.

Min.
  I did not like the sign, when Regulus,
  Whom all we know no friend unto Sejanus,
  Did, by Tiberius' so precise command,
  Succeed a fellow in the consulship:
  It boded somewhat.
Pom.
  Not a mote. His partner,
  Fulcinius Trio, is his own, and sure.———
  Here comes Terentius.
                Enter TERENTIUS.
  He can give us more.
            [They whisper with Terentius.
Lep.
  I'll ne'er believe, but Caesar hath some scent
  Of bold Sejanus' footing. These cross points
  Of varying letters, and opposing consuls,
  Mingling his honours and his punishments,

Feigning now ill, now well, raising Sejanus,
And then depressing him, as now of late
In all reports we have it, cannot be
Empty of practice: 'tis Tiberius' art.
For having found his favourite grown too great,
And with his greatness strong; that all the soldiers
Are, with their leaders, made a his devotion;
That almost all the senate are his creatures,
Or hold on him their main dependencies,
Either for benefit, or hope, or fear;
And that himself hath lost much of his own,
By parting unto him; and, by th' increase
Of his rank lusts and rages, quite disarm'd
Himself of love, or other public means,
To dare an open contestation;
His subtilty hath chose this doubling line,
To hold him even in: not so to fear him,
As wholly put him out, and yet give check
Unto his farther boldness. In mean time,
By his employments, makes him odious
Unto the staggering rout, whose aid, in fine,
He hopes to use, as sure, who, when they sway.
Bear down, o'erturn all objects in their way.

Arr.
  You may be a Lynceus, Lepidus: yet I
See no such cause, but that a politic tyrant,
Who can so well disguise it, should have ta'en
A nearer way: feign'd honest, and come home
To cut his throat, by law.

Lep.
  Ay, but his fear
Would ne'er be mask'd, allbe his vices were.

Pom. His lordship then is still in grace?

Ter.
  Assure you,
Never in more, either of grace or power.

Pom. The gods are wise and just.

Arr.
  The fiends they are,
To suffer thee belie 'em.

Ter.
  I have here

His last and present letters, where he writes him,
The partner of his cares, and his Sejanus.——

Lac.
But is that true? it is prohibited
To sacrifice unto him?

Ter.
Some such thing
Caesar makes scruple of, but forbids it not;
No more than to himself: says he could wish
It were forborn to all.

Lac. Is it no other?

Ter.
No other, on my trust. For your more surety,
Here is that letter too.

Arr.
How easily
Do wretched men believe, what they would have!
Looks this like plot?

Lep. Noble Arruntius, stay.

Lac. He names him here without his titles.

Lep. Note!

Arr. Yes, and come off your notable fool. I will

Lac. No other than Sejanus.

Pom.
That's but haste
In him that writes: here he gives large amends.

Mar. And with his own hand written?

Pom. Yes.

Lac. Indeed?

Ter.
Believe it, gentlemen, Sejanus' breast
Never received more full contentments in,
Than at this present.

Pom.
> Takes he well the escape
> Of young Caligula, with Macro?

Ter.
> Faith,
> At the first air it somewhat troubled him.

Lep. Observe you?

Arr.
> Nothing; riddles. Till I see
> Sejanus struck, no sound thereof strikes me.

[Exeunt Arrun. and Lepidus.

Pom.
> I like it not. I muse he would not attempt
> Somewhat against him in the consulship,
> Seeing the people 'gin to favour him.

Ter.
> He doth repent it now; but he has employ'd
> Pagonianus after him: and he holds
> That correspondence there, with all that are
> Near about Caesar, as no thought can pass
> Without his knowledge, thence in act to front him.

Pom. I gratulate the news.

Lac.
> But how comes Macro
> So in trust and favour with Caligula?

Pom.
> O, sir, he has a wife; and the young prince
> An appetite: he can look up, and spy
> Flies in the roof, when there are fleas i' the bed;
> And hath a learned nose to assure his sleeps.
> Who to be favour'd of the rising sun,
> Would not lend little of his waning moon?
> It is the saf'st ambition. Noble Terentius!

Ter. The night grows fast upon us. At your service.   [Exeunt.

ACT V

SCENE I.-An Apartment in SEJANUS' House.
Enter SEJANUS.

Sej.
  Swell, swell, my joys; and faint not to declare
  Yourselves as ample as your causes are.
  I did not live till now; this my first hour;
  Wherein I see my thoughts reach'd by my power.
  But this, and gripe my wishes. Great and high,
  The world knows only two, that's Rome and I.
  My roof receives me not; 'tis air I tread;
  And, at each step, I feel my advanced head
  Knock out a star in heaven! rear'd to this height,
  All my desires seem modest, poor, and slight,
  That did before sound impudent: 'tis place,
  Not blood, discerns the noble and the base.
  Is there not something more than to be Caesar?
  Must we rest there'! it irks t' have come so far,
  To be so near a stay. Caligula,
  Would thou stood'st stiff, and many in our way!
  Winds lose their strength, when they do empty fly,
  Unmet of woods or buildings; great fires die,
  That want their matter to withstand them: so,
  It is our grief, and will be our loss, to know
  Our power shall want opposites; unless
  The gods, by mixing in the cause, would bless
  Our fortune with their conquest. That were worth
  Sejanus' strife; durst fates but bring it forth.
                    Enter TERENTIUS.

Ter. Safety to great Sejanus!

Sej. Now, Terentius?

Ter. Hears not my lord the wonder?

Sej. Speak it, no.

Ter.
  I meet it violent in the people's mouths,
  Who run in routs to Pompey's theatre,
  To view your statue, which, they say, sends forth
  A smoke, as from a furnace, black and dreadful.

Sej.
  Some traitor hath put fire in: you, go see,

    And let the head be taken oft', to look
    What 'tis. [Exit Terentius.]——
    Some slave hath practised an imposture,
    To stir the people.-How now! why return you?

           Reenter TERENTIUS, with SATRIUS and NATTA.

Sat.
    The head, my lord, already is ta'en off,
    I saw it; and, at opening, there leapt out
    A great and monstrous serpent.

Sej.
    Monstrous! why?
    Had it a beard, and horns? no heart? a tongue
    Forked as flattery? look'd it of the hue,
    To such as live in great men's bosoms? was
    The spirit of it Macro's?

Nat.
    May it please
    The most divine Sejanus, in my days,
    (And by his sacred fortune, I affirm it,)
    I have not seen a more extended, grown,
    Foul, spotted, venomous, ugly——

Sej.
    O, the fates!
    What a wild muster's here of attributes,
    T'' express a worm, a snake!

Ter.
    But how that should
    Come there, my lord!

Sej.
    What, and you too, Terentius!
    I think you mean to make 't a prodigy
    In your reporting.

Ter. Can the wise Sejanus
    Think heaven hath meant it less!

Sej.
    O, superstition!
    Why, then the falling of our bed, that brake
    This morning, burden'd with the populous weight,
    Of our expecting clients, to salute us;
    Or running of the cat betwixt our legs,
    As we set forth unto the Capitol, Were prodigies.

Ter.
I think them ominous;
And would they had not happened! As, to-day,
The fate of some your servants: who, declining
Their way, not able, for the throng, to follow,
Slipt down the Gemonies, and brake their necks!
Besides, in taking your last augury,
No prosperous bird appear'd; but croaking ravens
Flagg'd up and down, and from the sacrifice
Flew to the prison, where they sat all night,
Beating the air with their obstreperous beaks!
I dare not counsel, but I could entreat,
That great Sejanus would attempt the gods
Once more with sacrifice.

Sej.
What excellent fools
Religion makes of men! Believes Terentius,
If these were dangers, as I shame to think them,
The gods could change the certain course of fate!
Or, if they could they would, now in a moment,
For a beeve's fat, or less, be bribed to invert
Those long decrees? Then think the gods, like flies,
Are to be taken with the steam of flesh,
Or blood, diffused about their altars: think
Their power as cheap as I esteem it small.——
Of all the throng that fill th' Olympian hall,
And, without pity, lade poor Atlas' back,
I know not that one deity, but Fortune,
To whom I would throw up, in begging smoke,
One grain of incense; or whose ear I'd buy
With thus much oil. Her I, indeed, adore;
And keep her grateful image in my house,
Sometime belonging to a Roman king.
But now call'd mine, as by the better style:
To her I care not, if, for satisfying
Your scrupulous phant'sies, I go offer. Bid
Our priest prepare us honey, milk, and poppy,
His masculine odours, and night-vestments: say,
Our rites are instant; which perform'd, you'll see
How vain, and worthy laughter, your fears be. [*Exeunt*

SCENE II.-Another Room in the same.
Enter COTTA and POMPONIUS.

Cot. Pomponius, whither in such speed?

Pom.
I go

  To give my lord Sejanus notice——

Cot. What?

Pom. Of Macro.

Cot. Is he come?

Pom.
 Enter'd but now
 The house of Regulus

Cot. The opposite consul!

Pom. Some half hour since.

Cot.
 And by night too! Stay, sir;
 I'll bear you company.

Pom. Along then——   [Exeunt
   SCENE III.-A Room in REGULUS'S House.
   Enter MACRO, REGULUS, and Attendant.

Mac.
 Tis Caesar's will to have a frequent senate;
 And therefore must your edict lay deep mulct
 On such as shall be absent.

Reg.
 So it doth.
 Bear it my fellow consul to adscribe.

Mac.
 And tell him it must early be proclaim'd:
 The place Apollo's temple.   [Exit Attendant

Reg. That's remember'd.

Mac. And at what hour!

Reg. Yes.

Mac.
 You do forget
 To send one for the provost of the watch.

Reg. I have not: here he comes.
       Enter LACO.

Mac.
　Gracinus Laco,
　You are a friend most welcome: by and by,
　I'll speak with you.——You must procure this list
　Of the praetorian cohorts, with the names
　Of the centurions, and their tribunes.

Reg. Ay.

Mac. I bring you letters, and a health from Caesar——

Lac. Sir, both come well.

Mac.
　And hear you? with your note,
　Which are the eminent men, and most of action.

Reg. That shall be done you too.

Mac.
　Most worthy Laco,
　Caesar salutes you.——　　　　　　　[Exit Regulus.]
　　　　　Consul! death and furies!
　Gone now!——The argument will please you, sir.
　Ho! Regulus! The anger of the gods
　Follow your diligent legs, and overtake 'em,
　In likeness of the gout!——
　　　　　　[Re-enter REGULUS.
　　　　　O, my good lord,
　We lack'd you present; I would pray you send
　Another to Fulcinius Trio, straight,
　To tell him you will come, and speak with him:
　The matter we'll devise, to stay him there,
　While I with Laco do survey the watch.　　[Exit Regulus.
　What are your strengths, Gracinus?

Lac. Seven cohorts.

Mac.
　You see what Caesar writes; and——Gone again!
　H' has sure a vein of mercury in his feet.——
　Know you what store of the praetorian soldiers
　Sejanus holds about him, for his guard?

Lac.
　I cannot the just number; but, I think,
　Three centuries.

Mac. Three! good.

Lac. At most not four.

Mac. And who be those centurions?

Lac.
  That the consul
  Can best deliver you.

Mac.
  When he's away!
  Spite on his nimble industry——Gracinus,
  You find what place you hold. there, in the trust
  Of royal Caesar?

Lac. Ay, and I am——

Mac.
  Sir,
  The honours there proposed are but beginnings
  Of his great favours.

Lac. They are more——

Mac.
  I heard him
  When he did study what to add.

Lac.
  My life,
  And all I hold——

Mac.
  You were his own first choice:
  Which doth confirm as much as you can speak;
  And will, if we succeed, make more——Your guards
  Are seven cohorts, you say?

Lac. Yes.

Mac.
  Those we must
  Hold still in readiness and undischarged.

Lac. I understand so much. But how it can——

Mac. Be done without suspicion, you'll object?
     Re-enter REGULUS.
Reg. What's that?

Lac.
>The keeping of the watch in arms,
>When morning comes.

Mac.
>The senate shall be met, and set
>So early in the temple, as all mark
>Of that shall be avoided.

Reg.
>If we need,
>We have commission to possess the palace,
>Enlarge prince Drusus, and make him our chief.

Mac.
>That secret would have burnt his reverend mouth,
>Had he not spit it out now: by the gods,
>You carry things too——Let me borrow a man
>Or two, to bear these——That of freeing Drusus,
>Caesar projected as the last and utmost;
>Not else to be remember'd.
>   Enter Servants.

Reg. Here are servants.

Mac.
>These to Arruntius, these to Lepidus;
>This bear to Cotta, this to Latiaris.
>If they demand you of me, say I have ta'en
>Fresh horse, and am departed.   [Exeunt Servants.
>   You, my lord,
>To your colleague, and be you sure to hold him
>With long narration of the new fresh favours,
>Meant to Sejanus, his great patron; I,
>With trusted Laco, here, are for the guards:
>Then to divide. For, night hath many eyes,
>Whereof, though most do sleep, yet some are spies.   [Exeunt
>   SCENE IV.—A Sacellum (or Chapel) in SEJANUS'S House.
>   Enter Praecones, Flamen, Tubicines, Tibicines, Ministri,
>   SEJANUS, TERENTIUS, SATRIUS, NATTA, etc.

Prae.
>Be all profane far hence; fly, fly far off:
>Be absent far; far hence be all profane!
>   [Tub. and Tib. sound while the Flamen washeth.

Fla.
>We have been faulty, but repent us now,
>And bring pure hands, pure vestments, and pure minds.

1 Min. Pure vessels.

2 Min. And pure offerings.

3 Min. Garlands pure.

Fla.
  Bestow your garlands: and, with reverence, place
  The vervin on the altar.

Prae. Favour your tongues.
[While they sound again, the Flamen takes of the honey with his finger, and tastes, then ministers to all the rest; so of the milk, in an earthen vessel, he deals about; which done, he sprinkleth upon the altar, milk; then imposeth the honey, and kindleth his gums, and after censing about the altar, placeth his censer thereon, into which they put several branches of poppy, and the music ceasing, proceeds.

Fla.
  Great mother Fortune, queen of human state,
  Redress of action, arbitress of fate,
  To whom all sway, all power, all empire bows,
  Be present; and propitious to our vows!

Prae. Favour it with your tongues.

Min. Be present and propitious to our vows!

Omnes. Accept our offering and be pleased, great goddess.

Ter. See, see, the image stirs!

Sat. And turns away!

Nat. Fortune averts her face.

Fla.
  Avert, you gods,
  The prodigy. Still! still, some pious rite
  We have neglected. Yet, heaven be appeased,
  And be all tokens false and void, that speak
  Thy present wrath!

Sej.
  Be thou dumb, scrupulous priest:
  And gather up thyself, with these thy wares
  Which I, in spite of thy blind mistress, or
  Thy juggling mystery, religion, throw

Thus scorned on the earth.
[Overturns the statue and the altar.

     Nay, hold thy look
Averted till I woo thee turn again
And thou shalt stand to all posterity,
The eternal game and laughter, with thy neck
Writh'd to thy tail, like a ridiculous cat.
Avoid these fumes, these superstitious lights,
And all these cozening ceremonies: you,
Your pure and spiced conscience!
 [Exeunt all but Sejanus, Terent., Satri., and Natta.

     I, the slave
And mock of fools, scorn on my worthy head!
That have been titled and adored a god,
Yea, sacrificed unto, myself, in Rome,
No less than Jove: and I be brought to do
A peevish giglot, rites! perhaps the thought
And shame of that, made fortune turn her face,
Knowing herself the lesser deity,
And but my servant.-Bashful queen, if so,
Sejanus thanks thy modesty.——Who's that?
    Enter POMPONIUS and MINUTIUS.

Pom.
 His fortune suffers, till he hears my news:
 I have waited here too long. Macro, my lord——

Sej. Speak lower and withdraw.   [Takes him aside.

Ter. Are these things true?

Min. Thousands are gazing at it in the streets.

Sej. What's that?

Ter.
 Minutius tells us here, my lord,
 That a new head being set upon your statue,
 A rope is since found wreath'd about it! and,
 But now a fiery meteor in the form
 Of a great ball was seen to roll along
 The troubled air, where yet it hangs unperfect,
 The amazing wonder of the multitude!

Sej. No more. That Macro's come, is more than all!

Ter. Is Macro come?

Pom. I saw him.

Ter. Where? with whom?

Pom. With Regulus.

Sej. Terentius!

Per. My lord.

Sej.
   Send for the tribunes, we will straight have up
More of the soldiers for our guard. [Exit Per.] Minutius,
We pray you go for Cotta, Latiaris,
Trio, the consul, or what senators
You know are sure, and ours. [Exit Min.] You, my good Natta,
For Laco, provost of the watch. [Exit Nat.] Now, Satrius,
The time of proof comes on; arm all our servants,
And without tumult. [Exit Sat.] You, Pomponius,
Hold some good correspondence with the consul:
Attempt him, noble friend. [Exit Pomp.] These things begin
To look like dangers, now, worthy my fates.
Fortune, I see thy worst: let doubtful states,
And things uncertain, hang upon thy will:
Me surest death shall render certain still.
Yet, why is now my thought turn'd toward death,
Whom fates have let go on, so far in breath,
Uncheck'd or unreproved? I that did help
To fell the lofty cedar of the world,
Germanicus; that at one stroke cut down
Drusus, that upright elm; wither'd his vine;
Laid Silius and Sabinus, two strong oaks,
Flat on the earth; besides those other shrubs,
Cordus and Sosia, Claudia Pulchra,
Furnius and Gallus, which I have grubb'd up;
And since, have set my axe so strong and deep
Into the root of spreading Agrippina;
Lopt off and scatter'd her proud branches,
Nero. Drusus; and Caius too, although re-planted.
If you will, Destinies, that after all,
I faint now ere I touch my period,
You are but cruel; and I already have done
Things great enough. All Rome hath been my slave;
The senate sate an idle looker on,
And witness of my power; when I have blush'd
More to command than it to suffer: all
The fathers have sate ready and prepared.
To give me empire, temples, or their throats.

When I would ask 'em; and what crowns the top,
Rome, senate, people, all the world have seen
Jove, but my equal; Caesar, but my second.
'Tis then your malice, Fates, who, but your own,
Envy and fear to have any power long known.

SCENE V.——A Room in the same.

Enter TERENTIUS and Tribunes.

Ter. Stay here: I'll give his lordship, you are come.

Enter MINUTIUS, with COTTA and LATIARIS.

Min.
Marcus Terentius, 'pray you tell my lord
Here's Cotta, and Latiaris.

Ter. Sir, I shall.

Cot.
My letter is the very same with yours;
Only requires me to be present there,
And give my voice to strengthen his design.

Lat. Names he not what it is?

Cot. No, nor to you.

Lat. 'Tis strange and singular doubtful!

Cot.
So it is.
It may be all is left to lord Sejanus.

Enter NATTA and GRACINUS LACO.

Nat. Gentlemen, where's my lord?

Tri. We wait him here.

Cot. The provost Laco! what's the news?

Lat. My lord——

Enter SEJANUS.

Sej.
Now, my right dear, noble, and trusted friends,
How much I am a captive to your kindness!
Most worthy Cotta, Latiaris, Laco,
Your valiant hand; and, gentlemen, your loves.
I wish I could divide myself unto you;

Or that it lay within our narrow powers,
To satisfy for so enlarged bounty.
Gracinus, we must pray you, hold your guards
Unquit when morning comes. Saw you the consul?

Min. Trio will presently be here, my lord.

Cot.
They are but giving order for the edict,
To warn the senate.

Sej. How! the senate?

Lac.
Yes.
This morning in Apollo's temple.

Cot.
We
Are charged by letter to be there, my lord.

Sej. By letter! pray you, let's see.

Lat. Knows not his lordship?

Cot. It seems so!

Sej.
A senate warn'd! Without my knowledge!
And on this sudden! Senators by letters
Required to be there! who brought these?

Cot. Macro.

Sej. Mine enemy! and when?

Cot. This midnight.

Sej.
Time,
With every other circumstance, doth give
It hath some strain of engine in't!——How now?
      Enter SATRIUS.
Sat.
My lord, Sertorius Macro is without,
Alone, and prays t' have private conference
In business of high nature with your lordship,
He says to me, and which regards you much.

Sej. Let him come here.

Sat.
  Better, my lord, Withdraw:
  You will betray what store and strength of friends
  Are now about you; which he comes to spy.

Sej. Is he not arm'd?

Sat. We'll search him.

Sej.
  No; but take,
  And lead him to some room, where you conceal'd
  May keep a guard upon us.   [Exit Sat.]
          Noble Laco,
  You are our trust; and till our own cohorts
  Can be brought up, your strengths must be our guard.
  Now, good Minutius, honour'd Latiaris,
                        [He salutes them humbly.
  Most worthy and my most unwearied friends:
  I return instantly.   [Exit.

Lat. Most worthy lord.

Cot.
  His lordship is turn'd instant kind, methinks;
  I have not observed it in him, heretofore.

1 *Tri.* 'Tis true, and it becomes him nobly.

Min.
  I
  Am wrapt withal.

2 *Tri.*
  By Mars, he has my lives,
  Were they a million, for this only grace.

Lac. Ay, and to name a man!

Lat. As he did me!

Min. And me!

Lat.
  Who would not spend his life and fortunes,
  To purchase but the look of such a lord?
Lac.

He that would nor be lord's fool, nor the world's.   [Aside.
    SCENE VI.-Another Room in the same.
      Enter SEJANUS, MACRO, and SATRIUS.

Sej.
  Macro! most welcome, a most coveted friend!
  Let me enjoy my longings. When arrived you?

Mac. About the noon of night.

Sej. Satrius, give leave.   [Exit Sat.

Mac.
  I have been, since I came, with both the consuls,
  On a particular design from Caesar.

Sej. How fares it with our great and royal master?

Mac.
  Right plentifully well; as, with a prince,
  That still holds out the great proportion
  Of his large favours, where his judgment hath
  Made once divine election: like the god
  That wants not, nor is wearied to bestow
  Where merit meets his bounty, as it doth
  In you, already the most happy, and ere
  The sun shall climb the south, most high Sejanus.
  Let not my lord be amused. For, to this end
  Was I by Caesar sent for to the isle,
  With special caution to conceal my journey;
  And, thence, had my dispatch as privately
  Again to Rome; charged to come here by night;
  And only to the consuls make narration
  Of his great purpose; that the benefit
  Might come more full, and striking, by how much
  It was less look'd for, or aspired by you,
  Or least informed to the common thought.

Sej.
  What may be this? part of myself, dear Macro,
  If good, speak out; and share with your Sejanus.

Mac.
  If bad, I should for ever loath myself
  To be the messenger to so good a lord.
  I do exceed my instructions to acquaint
  Your lordship with thus much; but 'tis my venture
  On your retentive wisdom: and because
  I would no jealous scruple should molest

Or rack your peace of thought. For I assure
My noble lord, no senator yet knows
The business meant: though all by several letters
Are warned to be there, and give their voices,
Only to add unto the state and grace
Of what is purposed.

Sej.
   You take pleasure, Macro,
Like a coy wench, in torturing your lover.
What can be worth this suffering?

Mac.
   That which follows,
The tribunitial dignity and power:
Both which Sejanus is to have this day
Conferr'd upon him, and by public senate.

Sej.
   Fortune be mine again! thou hast satisfied
For thy suspected loyalty.   [Aside.

Mac.
   My lord,
I have no longer time, the day approacheth,
And I must back to Caesar.

Sej. Where's Caligula?

Mac.
   That I forgot to tell your lordship. Why,
He lingers yonder about Capreae,
Disgraced; Tiberius hath not seen him yet:
He needs would thrust himself to go with me,
Against my wish or will; but I have quitted
His forward trouble, with as tardy note
As my neglect or silence could afford him.
Your lordship cannot now command me aught,
Because I take no knowledge that I saw you;
But I shall boast to live to serve your lordship:
And so take leave.

Sej.
   Honest and worthy Macro;
Your love and friendship.   [Exit Macro.]
      ——Who's there? Satrius,
Attend my honourable friend forth.-O!
How vain and vile a passion is this fear,
What base uncomely things it makes men do!

Suspect their noblest friends, as I did this,
Flatter poor enemies, entreat their servants,
Stoop, court, and catch at the benevolence
Of creatures, unto whom, within this hour,
I would not have vouchsafed a quarter-look,
Or piece of face! By you that fools call gods,
Hang all the sky with your prodigious signs,
Fill earth with monsters, drop the scorpion down,
Out of the zodiac, or the fiercer lion,
Shake off the loosen'd globe from her long hinge,
Roll all the world in darkness, and let loose
The enraged winds to turn up groves and towns!
When I do fear again, let me be struck
With forked fire, and unpitied die:
Who fears, is worthy of calamity.   [Exit.
             SCENE VII.-Another Room in the same.

Enter TERENTIUS, MINUTIUS, LACO, COTTA, LATIARIS,
and POMPONIUS; REGULUS, TRIO, and others, on different sides.

Pom. Is not my lord here?

Ter. Sir, he will be straight.

Cot. What news, Fulcinius Trio?

Tri.
   Good, good tidings;
   But keep it to yourself. My lord Sejanus
   Is to receive this day in open senate
   The tribunitial dignity.

Cot. Is't true?

Tri. No words, not to your thought: but, sir, believe it.

Lat. What says the consul?

Cot.
   Speak it not again:
   He tells me, that to-day my lord Sejanus——

Tri.
   I must entreat you, Cotta, on your honour
   Not to reveal it.

Cot. On my life, sir.

Lat. Say.

Cot.
   Is to receive the tribunitial power.
   But, as you are an honourable man,
   Let me conjure you not to utter it;
   For it is trusted to me with that bond.

Lat. I am Harpocrates.

Ter. Can you assure it?

Pom. The consul told it me, but keep it close.

Min. Lord Latiaris, what's the news?

Lat.
   I'll tell you;
   But you must swear to keep it secret.
                              Enter SEJANUS.
Sej.
   I knew the Fates had on their distaff left
   More of our thread, than so.

Reg. Hail, great Sejanus!

Tri. Hail, the most honour'd!

Cot. Happy!

Lat. High Sejanus!

Sej. Do you bring prodigies too?

Tri.
   May all presage
   Turn to those fair effects, whereof we bring
   Your lordship news.

Reg. May't please my lord withdraw.

Sej. Yes:-I will speak with you anon.   [To some that stand by.

Ter.
   My lord,
   What is your pleasure for the tribunes?

Sej.
   Why,
   Let them be thank'd and sent away.

Min. My lord——

Lac. Will't please your lordship to command me-

Sej.
  No:
  You are troublesome.

Min. The mood is changed.

Tri.
  Not speak,
  Nor look!

Lac.
  Ay, he is wise, will make him friends
  Of such who never love, but for their ends.   [Exeunt.
      SCENE VIII.-A Space before the Temple of Apollo.
    Enter ARRUNTIUS and LEPIDUS divers Senators passing by them.
Arr.
  Ay, go, make haste; take heed you be not last
  To tender your All Hail in the wide hall
  Of huge Sejanus: run a lictor's pace:
  Stay, not to put your robes on; but away,
  With the pale troubled ensigns of great friendship
  Stamp'd in your face! Now, Marcus Lepidus,
  You still believe your former augury!
  Sejanus must go downward! You perceive
  His wane approaching fast!

Lep. Believe me, Lucius, I wonder at this rising.

Arr.
  Ay, and that we
  Must give our suffrage to it. You will say,
  It is to make his fall more steep and grievous:
  It may be so. But think it, they that can
  With idle wishes 'say to bring back time:
  In cases desperate, all hope is crime.
  See, see! what troops of his officious friends
  Flock to salute my lord, and start before
  My great proud lord! to get a lord-like nod!
  Attend my lord unto the senate-house!
  Bring back my lord! like servile ushers, make
  Way for my lord! proclaim his idol lordship,
  More than ten criers, or six noise of trumpets!
  Make legs, kiss hands, and take a scatter'd hair
  From my lord's eminent shoulder!

[*Sanquinius and Haterius pass over the stage.*
See, Sanquinius
With his slow belly, and his dropsy! look,
What toiling haste he makes! yet here's another
Retarded with the gout, will be afore him.
Get thee Liburnian porters, thou gross fool,
To bear thy obsequious fatness, like thy peers.
They are met! the gout returns, and his great carriage.
[*Lictors, Regulus, Trio, Sejanus, Satrius,
and many other Senators, pass over the stage.*

Lict. Give way, make place, room for the consul!

San.
  Hail,
  Hail, great. Sejanus!

Hat. Hail, my honour'd lord!

Arr. We shall be mark'd anon, for our not Hail.

Lep. That is already done.

Arr.
  It is a note
Of upstart greatness, to observe and watch
For these poor trifles, which the noble mind
Neglects and scorns.

Lep.
  Ay, and they think themselves
Deeply dishonour'd where they are omitted,
As if they were necessities that help'd
To the perfection of their dignities;
And hate the men that but refrain them.

Arr.
  O!
There is a farther cause of hate. Their breasts
Are guilty, that we know their obscure springs,
And base beginnings; thence the anger grows.
On. Follow.
          SCENE IX.-*Another part of the same.*
          Enter MACRO *and* LACO.

Mac.
  When all are enter'd, shut the temple doors;
And bring your guards up to the gate.

Lac. I will.

Mac.
  If you shall hear commotion in the senate,
  Present yourself: and charge on any man
  Shall offer to come forth.

Lac. I am instructed. [Exeunt.

SCENE X.-The Temple of Apollo.

Enter HATERIUS, TRIO, SANQUINIUS, COTTA, REGULUS, SEJANUS, POMPONIUS, LATIARIS, LEPIDUS, ARRUNTIUS, and divers other Senators; Praecones, and Lictors.

Hat. How well, his lordship looks to-day!

Tri.
  As if
  He had been born, or made for this hour's state.

Cat. Your fellow consul's come about, methinks?

Tri. Ay, he is wise.

San. Sejanus trusts him well.

Tri. Sejanus is a noble, bounteous lord.

Hat. He is so, and most valiant.

Lat. And most wise.

1 Sen. He's every thing.

Lat.
  Worthy of all, and more
  Than bounty can bestow.

Tri.
  This dignity
  Will make him worthy.

Pom. Above Caesar.

San.
  Tut,
  Caesar is but the rector of an isle,
  He of the empire.

Tri.
    Now he will have power
    More to reward than ever.

Cat.
    Let us look
    We be not slack in giving him our voices.

Lat. Not I.

San. Nor I.

Col.
    The readier we seem
    To propagate his honours, will more bind
    His thoughts to ours.

Hat.
    I think right with your lordship;
    It is the way to have us hold our places.

San. Ay, and get more.

Lat. More office and more titles.

Pom.
    I will not lose the part I hope to share I
    n these his fortunes, for my patrimony.

Lat. See, how Arruntius sits, and Lepidus!

Tri. Let them alone, they will be mark'd anon.

1 Sen. I'll do with others.

2 Sen. So will I.

3 Sen.
    And I.
    Men grow not in the state, but as they are planted
    Warm in his favours.

Col. Noble Sejanus!

Hat. Honour'd Sejanus!

Lat. Worthy and great Sejanus!

Arr.

   Gods! how the sponges open and take in,
   And shut again! look, look! is not he blest
   That gets a seat in eye-reach of him? more,
   That comes in ear, or tongue-reach? O but most,
   Can claw his subtle elbow, or with a buz
   Fly-blow his ears?

Praet. Proclaim the senate's peace,
   And give last summons by the edict.

Prae.
   Silence!
   In name of Caesar, and the senate, silence!
Memmius Regulus, and Fulcinius Trio, consuls, these present kalends
of June, with the first light, shall hold a senate, in the temple
of Apollo Palatine: all that are fathers, and are registered
fathers that have right of entering the senate, we warn or command
you be frequently present, take knowledge the business is the
commonwealth's: whosoever is absent, his fine or mulct will be
taken, his excuse will not be taken.

Tri. Note who are absent, and record their names.

Reg.
   Fathers conscript, may what I am to utter
   Turn good and happy for the commonwealth!
   And thou, Apollo, in whose holy house
   We here have met, inspire us all with truth,
   And liberty of censure to our thought!
   The majesty of great Tiberius Caesar
   Propounds to this grave senate, the bestowing
   Upon the man he loves, honour'd Sejanus,
   The tribunitial dignity and power:
   Here are his letters, signed with his signet.
   What pleaseth now the fathers to be done?

Sen. Read, read them, open, publicly read them.

Cot.
   Caesar hath honour'd his own greatness much
   In thinking of this act.

Tri.
   It was a thought
   Happy, and worthy Caesar.

Lat.
   And the lord
   As worthy it, on whom it is directed!

Hat. Most worthy!

San.
  Rome did never boast the virtue
  That could give envy bounds, but his: Sejanus——

1 Sen. Honour'd and noble!

2 Sen. Good and great Sejanus!

Arr. O, most tame slavery, and fierce flattery!

Prae. Silence!

     TIBERIUS CAESAR to the Senate, greeting.

If you, conscript fathers, with your children, be in health, it is
abundantly well: we with our friends here are so. The care of the
commonwealth, howsoever we are removed in person, cannot be absent
to our thought; although, oftentimes, even to princes most present,
the truth of their own affairs is hid, than which, nothing falls
out more miserable to a state, or makes the art of governing more
difficult. But since it hath been our easeful happiness to enjoy
both the aids and industry of so vigilant a senate, we profess to
have been the more indulgent to our pleasures, not as being
careless of our office, but rather secure of the necessity. Neither
do these common rumours of many, and infamous libels published
against our retirement, at all afflict us; being born more out of
men's ignorance than their malice: and will, neglected, find their
own grave quickly, whereas, too sensibly acknowledged, it would
make their obloquy ours. Nor do we desire their authors, though
found, be censured, since in a free state, as ours, all men ought
to enjoy both their minds and tongues free.

Arr. The lapwing, the lapwing!
Yet in things which shall worthily and more near concern the
majesty of a prince, we shall fear to be so unnaturally cruel to
our own fame, as to neglect them. True it is, conscript fathers,
that we have raised Sejanus from obscure, and almost unknown gentry

Sen. How, how!
to the highest and most conspicuous point of greatness, and, we
hope, deservingly, yet not without danger: it being a most bold
hazard in that sovereign, who, by his particular love to one, dares
adventure the hatred of all his other subjects.

Arr. This touches; the blood turns.
But we affy in your loves and understandings, and do no way suspect

the merit of our Sejanus, to make our favours offensive to any.

Sen. O! good, good.
Though we could have wished his zeal had run a calmer course
against Agrippina and our nephews, howsoever the openness of their
actions declared them delinquents, and, that he would have
remembered, no innocence is so safe, but it rejoiceth to stand in
the sight of mercy: the use of which in us, he hath so quite taken
away, towards them, by his loyal fury, as now our clemency would be
thought but wearied cruelty, if we should offer to exercise it.

Arr. I thank him; there I look'd for't. A good fox!
Some there be that would interpret this his public severity to be
particular ambition, and that, under a pretext of service to us, he
doth but remove his own lets: alleging the strengths he hath made
to himself, by the praetorian soldiers, by his faction in court and
senate, by the offices he holds himself, and confers on others, his
popularity and dependents, his urging and almost driving us to this
our unwilling retirement, and, lastly, his aspiring to be our
son-in-law.

Sen. This is strange!

Arr. I shall anon believe your vultures, Marcus.
Your wisdoms, conscript fathers, are able to examine, and censure
these suggestions. But, were they left to our absolving voice, we
durst pronounce them, as we think them, most malicious.

Sen. O, he has restored all; list!
   And give last summons by the edict.

Prae.
   Silence!
   In name of Caesar, and the senate, silence!
Memmius Regulus, and Fulcinius Trio, consuls, these present kalends
of June, with the first light, shall hold a senate, in the temple
of Apollo Palatine: all that are fathers, and are registered
fathers that have right of entering the senate, we warn or command
you be frequently present, take knowledge the business is the
commonwealth's: whosoever is absent, his fine or mulct will be
taken, his excuse will not be taken.

Tri. Note who are absent, and record their names.

Reg.
   Fathers conscript, may what I am to utter
   Turn good and happy for the commonwealth!
   And thou, Apollo, in whose holy house
   We here have met, inspire us all with truth,

And liberty of censure to our thought!
The majesty of great Tiberius Caesar
Propounds to this grave senate, the bestowing
Upon the man he loves, honour'd Sejanus,
The tribunitial dignity and power:
Here are his letters, signed with his signet.
What pleaseth now the fathers to be done?

Sen. Read, read them, open, publicly read them.

Cot.
Caesar hath honour'd his own greatness much
In thinking of this act.

Tri.
It was a thought
Happy, and worthy Caesar.

Lat.
And the lord
As worthy it, on whom it is directed!

Hat. Most worthy!

San.
Rome did never boast the virtue
That could give envy bounds, but his: Sejanus——

1 Sen. Honour'd and noble!

2 Sen. Good and great Sejanus!

Arr. O, most tame slavery, and fierce flattery!

Prae. Silence!

      TIBERIUS CAESAR to the Senate, greeting.

"If you, conscript fathers, with your children, be in health, it is
abundantly well: we with our friends here are so. The care of the
commonwealth, howsoever we are removed in person, cannot be absent
to our thought; although, oftentimes, even to princes most present,
the truth of their own affairs is hid, than which, nothing falls
out more miserable to a state, or makes the art of governing more
difficult. But since it hath been our easeful happiness to enjoy
both the aids and industry of so vigilant a senate, we profess to
have been the more indulgent to our pleasures, not as being
careless of our office, but rather secure of the necessity. Neither
do these common rumours of many, and infamous libels published

against our retirement, at all afflict us; being born more out of men's ignorance than their malice: and will, neglected, find their own grave quickly, whereas, too sensibly acknowledged, it would make their obloquy ours. Nor do we desire their authors, though found, be censured, since in a free state, as ours, all men ought to enjoy both their minds and tongues free."

Arr. The lapwing, the lapwing!

"Yet in things which shall worthily and more near concern the majesty of a prince, we shall fear to be so unnaturally cruel to our own fame, as to neglect them. True it is, conscript fathers, that we have raised Sejanus from obscure, and almost unknown gentry"

Sen. How, how!

"to the highest and most conspicuous point of greatness, and, we hope, deservingly, yet not without danger: it being a most bold hazard in that sovereign, who, by his particular love to one, dares adventure the hatred of all his other subjects."

Arr. This touches; the blood turns.

"But we affy in your loves and understandings, and do no way suspect the merit of our Sejanus, to make our favours offensive to any."

Sen. O! good, good.

"Though we could have wished his zeal had run a calmer course against Agrippina and our nephews, howsoever the openness of their actions declared them delinquents, and, that he would have remembered, no innocence is so safe, but it rejoiceth to stand in the sight of mercy: the use of which in us, he hath so quite taken away, towards them, by his loyal fury, as now our clemency would be thought but wearied cruelty, if we should offer to exercise it."

Arr. I thank him; there I look'd for't. A good fox!

"Some there be that would interpret this his public severity to be particular ambition, and that, under a pretext of service to us, he doth but remove his own lets: alleging the strengths he hath made to himself, by the praetorian soldiers, by his faction in court and senate, by the offices he holds himself, and confers on others, his popularity and dependents, his urging and almost driving us to this our unwilling retirement, and, lastly, his aspiring to be our son-in-law."

Sen. This is strange!

Arr. I shall anon believe your vultures, Marcus.

"Your wisdoms, conscript fathers, are able to examine, and censure these suggestions. But, were they left to our absolving voice, we durst pronounce them, as we think them, most malicious."

Sen. O, he has restored all; list!

"Yet are they offered to be averred, and on the lives of the informers. What we should say, or rather what we should not say, lords of the senate, if this be true, our gods and goddesses confound us if we know! Only we must think, we have placed our benefits ill; and conclude, that in our choice, either we were wanting to the gods, or the gods to us."
                    [The Senators shift their places.

Arr. The place grows hot; they shift.

"We have not been covetous, honourable fathers, to change, neither is it now any new lust that alters our affection, or old lothing, but those needful jealousies of state, that warn wiser princes hourly to provide their safety, and do teach them how learned a thing it is to beware of the humblest enemy; much more of those great ones, whom their own employed favours have made fit for their fears."

1 Sen. Away.

2 Sen. Sit farther.

Cot. Let's remove—

Arr. Gods! how the leaves drop off, this little wind!

"We therefore desire, that the offices he holds be first seized by the senate, and himself suspended from all exercise of place or power—"

Sen. How!

San. [thrusting by.] By your leave.

Arr.
   Come, porpoise; where's Haterius?
   His gout keeps him most miserably constant;
   Your dancing shews a tempest.

Sej. Read no more.

Reg. Lords of the senate, hold your seats: read on.

Sej. These letters they are forged.

Reg. A guard! sit still.
Enter LACO, with the Guards.
Arr. Here's change!

Reg. Bid silence, and read forward.

Prae. Silence!——

"and himself suspended from all exercise of place or power, but till due and mature trial be made of his innocency, which yet we can faintly apprehend the necessity to doubt. If, conscript fathers, to your more searching wisdoms, there shall appear farther cause——or of farther proceeding, either to seizure of lands, goods, or more——it is not our power that shall limit your authority, or our favour that must corrupt your justice: either were dishonourable in you, and both uncharitable to ourself. We would willingly be present with your counsels in this business, but the danger of so potent a faction, if it should prove so, forbids our attempting it: except one of the consuls would be entreated for our safety, to undertake the guard of us home; then we should most readily adventure. In the mean time, it shall not be fit for us to importune so judicious a senate, who know how much they hurt the innocent, that spare the guilty; and how grateful a sacrifice to the gods is the life of an ingrateful person, We reflect not, in this, on Sejanus, (notwithstanding, if you keep an eye upon him-and there is Latiaris, a senator, and Pinnarius Natta, two of his most trusted ministers, and so professed, whom we desire not to have apprehended,) but as the necessity of the cause exacts it."

Reg. A guard on Latiaris!

Arr.
  O, the spy,
  The reverend spy is caught! who pities him?
  Reward, sir, for your service: now, you have done
  Your property, you see what use is made!
[Exeunt Latiaris and Natta, guarded.
  Hang up the instrument.

Sej. Give leave.

Lac.
  Stand, stand!

He comes upon his 'death, that doth advance
An inch toward my point.

Sej. Have we no friends here?

Arr.
 Hush'd!
 Where now are all the hails and acclamations?
                                                    Enter MACRO.
Mac. Hail to the consuls, and this noble senate!

Sej.
 Is Macro here?
  O, thou art lost, Sejanus!   [Aside.

Mac.
 Sit still, and unaffrighted, reverend fathers:
 Macro, by Caesar's grace, the new-made provost,
 And now possest of the praetorian bands,
 An honour late belong'd to that proud man,
 Bids you be safe: and to your constant doom
 Of his deservings, offers you the surety
 Of all the soldiers, tribunes, and centurions,
 Received in our command.

Reg. Sejanus, Sejanus, Stand forth, Sejanus!

Sej. Am I call'd?

Mac.
 Ay, thou,
 Thou insolent monster, art bid stand.

Sej.
 Why, Macro.
 It hath been otherwise between you and I;
 This court, that knows us both, hath seen a difference,
 And can, if it be pleased to speak, confirm
 Whose insolence is most.

Mac.
 Come down, Typhoeus.
 If mine be most, lo! thus I make it more;
 Kick up thy heels in air, tear off thy robe,
 Play with thy beard and nostrils. Thus 'tis fit
 (And no man take compassion of thy state)
 To use th' ingrateful viper, tread his brains
 Into the earth.

Reg. Forbear.

Mac.
  If I could lose
All my humanity now, 'twere well to torture
So meriting a traitor.-Wherefore, fathers,
Sit you amazed and silent; and not censure
This wretch, who, in the hour he first rebell'd
'Gainst Caesar's bounty, did condemn himself?
Phlegra, the field where all the sons of earth
Muster'd against the gods, did ne'er acknowledge
So proud and huge a monster.

Reg.
  Take him hence;
And all the gods guard Caesar!

Tri. Take him hence.

Hat. Hence.

Cot. To the dungeon with him.

San. He deserves it.

Sen. Crown all our doors with bays.

San.
  And let an ox,
With gilded horns and garlands, straight be led
Unto the Capitol——

Hat.
  And sacrificed
To Jove, for Caesar's safety.

Tri.
  All our gods
Be present still to Caesar!

Cot. Phoebus.

San. Mars.

Hat. Diana.

San. Pallas.

Sen.

Juno, Mercury,
   All guard him!

Mac. Forth, thou prodigy of men!   [*Exit Sejanus, guarded.*

Cot. Let all the traitor's titles be defaced.

Tri. His images and statues be pull'd down.

Hat. His chariot-wheels be broken.

Arr.
   And the legs
   Of the poor horses, that deseryed nought,
   Let them be broken too!

      [*Exeunt Lictors, Praecones, Macro, Regulus, Trio,
      Haterius, and Sanquinius: manent Lepidus, Arruntius,
      and a few Senators.*

Lep.
   O violent change,
   And whirl of men's affections!

Arr.
   Like, as both
   Their bulks and souls were bound on Fortune's wheel,
   And must act only with her motion.

Lep.
   Who would depend upon the popular air,
   Or voice of men, that have to-day beheld
   That which, if all the gods had fore-declared,
   Would not have been believed, Sejanus' fall?
   He, that this morn rose proudly, as the sun,
   And, breaking through a mist of clients' breath,
   Came on, as gazed at and admired as he,
   When superstitious Moors salute his light!
   That had our servile nobles waiting him
   As common grooms; and hanging on his look,
   No less than human life on destiny!
   That had men's knees as frequent as the gods;
   And sacrifices more than Rome had altars:
   And this man fall! fall? ay, without a look
   That durst appear his friend, or lend so much
   Of vain relief, to his changed state, as pity!

Arr.
   They that before, like gnats, play'd in his beams,

And throng'd to circumscribe him, now not seen
Nor deign to hold a common seat with him!
Others, that waited him unto the senate,
Now inhumanely ravish him to prison,
Whom, but this morn, they follow'd as their lord!
Guard through the streets, bound like a fugitive,
Instead of wreaths give fetters, strokes for stoops,
Blind shames for honours, and black taunts for titles!
Who would trust slippery chance?

Lep.
They that would make
Themselves her spoil; and foolishly forget,
When she doth flatter, that she comes to prey.
Fortune, thou hadst no deity, if men
Had wisdom: we have placed thee so high,
By fond belief in thy felicity.
              [Shout within.] The gods guard Caesar!
                   All the gods guard Caesar!

Re-enter MACRO, REGULUS, and divers Senators.

Mac.
Now, great Sejanus, you that awed the state,
And sought to bring the nobles to your whip;
That would be Caesar's tutor, and dispose
Of dignities and offices! that had
The public head still bare to your designs,
And made the general voice to echo yours!
That look'd for salutations twelve score off,
And would have pyramids, yea temples, rear'd
To your huge greatness; now you lie as flat,
As was your pride advanced!

Reg. Thanks to the gods!

Sen.
And praise to Macro, that hath saved Rome!
Liberty, liberty, liberty! Lead on,
And praise to Macro, that hath saved Rome!
              [Exeunt all but Arruntius and Lepidus.

Arr.
I prophesy, out of the senate's flattery,
That this new fellow, Macro, will become
A greater prodigy in Rome, than he
That now is fallen.
                   Enter TERENTIUS.

Ter.
>   O you, whose minds are good,
>   And have not forced all mankind from your breasts;
>   That yet have so much stock of virtue left,
>   To pity guilty states, when they are wretched:
>   Lend your soft ears to hear, and eyes to weep,
>   Deeds done by men, beyond the acts of furies.
>   The eager multitude (who never yet
>   Knew why to love or hate, but only pleased
>   T' express their rage of power) no sooner heard
>   The murmur of Sejanus in decline,
>   But with that speed and heat of appetite,
>   With which they greedily devour the way
>   To some great sports, or a new theatre,
>   They fill'd the Capitol, and Pompey's Cirque,
>   Where, like so many mastiffs, biting stones,
>   As if his statues now were sensitive
>   Of their wild fury; first, they tear them down;
>   Then fastening ropes, drag them along the streets,
>   Crying in scorn, This, this was that rich head
>   Was crown'd with garlands, and with odours, this
>   That was in Rome so reverenced! Now
>   The furnace and the bellows shall to work,
>   The great Sejanus crack, and piece by piece
>   Drop in the founder's pit.

Lep. O popular rage!

Ter.
>   The whilst the senate at the temple of Concord
>   Make haste to meet again, and thronging cry,
>   Let us condemn him, tread him down in water,
>   While he doth lie upon the bank; away!
>   While some more tardy, cry unto their bearers,
>   He will be censured ere we come; run, knaves,
>   And use that furious diligence, for fear
>   Their bondmen should inform against their slackness,
>   And bring their quaking flesh unto the hook:
>   The rout they follow with confused voice,
>   Crying, they're glad, say, they could ne'er abide him,
>   Enquire what man he was, what kind of face,
>   What beard he had, what nose, what lips?
>   Protest They ever did presage he'd come to this;
>   They never thought him wise, nor valiant; ask
>   After his garments, when he dies, what death;
>   And not a beast of all the herd demands,
>   What was his crime, or who were his accusers,
>   Under what proof or testimony he fell?
>   There came, says one, a huge long-worded letter

From Capreae against him. Did there so?
O, they are satisfied; no more.

Lep. Alas!
   They follow Fortune, and hate men condemn'd,
   Guilty or not.

Arr.
   But had Sejanus thrived
   In his design, and prosperously opprest
   The old Tiberius; then, in that same minute,
   These very rascals, that now rage like furies,
   Would have proclaim'd Sejanus emperor.

Lep. But what hath follow'd?

Ter.
   Sentence by the senate,
   To lose his head; which was no sooner off,
   But that and the unfortunate trunk were seized
   By the rude multitude; who not content
   With what the forward justice of the state.
   Officiously had done, with violent rage
   Have rent it limb from limb. A thousand heads,
   A thousand hands, ten thousand tongues and voices,
   Employ'd at once in several acts of malice!
   Old men not staid with age, virgins with shame,
   Late wives with loss of husbands, mothers of children,
   Losing all grief in joy of his sad fall,
   Run quite transported with their cruelty!
   These mounting at his head, these at his face,
   These digging out his eyes, those with his brains
   Sprinkling themselves, their houses and their friends;
   Others are met, have ravish'd thence an arm,
   And deal small pieces of the flesh for favours;
   These with a thigh, this hath cut off his hands,
   And this his feet; these fingers and these toes;
   That hath his liver, he his heart: there wants
   Nothing but room for wrath, and place for hatred!
   What cannot oft be done, is now o'erdone.
   The whole, and all of what was great Sejanus,
   And, next to Caesar, did possess the World,
   Now torn and scatter'd, as he needs no grave;
   Each little dust covers a little part:
   So lies he no where, and yet often buried!
                           Enter NUNTIUS
Arr. More of Sejanus

Nun. Yes.

Lep.
   What can be added?
   We know him dead.

Nun.
   Then there begin your pity.
   There is enough behind to melt ev'n Rome,
   And Caesar into tears; since never slave
   Could yet so highly offend, but tyranny,
   In torturing him, would make him worth lamenting.——
   A son and daughter to the dead Sejanus,
   (Of whom there is not now so much remaining
   As would give fast'ning to the hangman's hook,)
   Have they drawn forth for farther sacrifice;
   Whose tenderness of knowledge, unripe years,
   And childish silly innocence was such,
   As scarce would lend them feeling of their danger:
   The girl so simple, as she often ask'd
   "Where they would lead her? for what cause they dragg'd her?"
   Cried, "She would do no more:" that she could take
   "Warning with beating." And because our laws
   Admit no virgin immature to die,
   The wittily and strangely cruel Macro
   Deliver'd her to be deflower'd and spoil'd,
   By the rude lust of the licentious hangman,
   Then to be strangled with her harmless brother.

Lep.
   O, act most worthy hell, and lasting night,
   To hide it from the world!

Nun.
   Their bodies thrown
   Into the Gemonies, (I know not how,
   Or by what accident return'd.) the mother,
   The expulsed Apicata, finds them there;
   Whom when she saw lie spread on the degrees,
   After a world of fury on herself,
   Tearing her hair, defacing of her face,
   Beating her breasts and womb, kneeling amaz'd,
   Crying to heaven, then to them; at last,
   Her drowned voice gat up above her woes,
   And with such black and bitter execrations,
   As might affright the gods, and force the sun
   Run backward to the east; nay, make the old
   Deformed chaos rise again, to o'erwhelm
   Them, us, and all the world, she fills the air,
   Upbraids the heavens with their partial dooms,

    Defies their tyrannous powers, and demands,
    What she, and those poor innocents have transgress'd,
    That they must suffer such a share in vengeance,
    Whilst Livia, Lygdus, and Eudemus live,
    Who, as she says, and firmly vows to prove it
    To Caesar and the senate, poison'd Drusus?

Lup. Confederates with her husband!

Nun. Ay.

Lep. Strange act!

Arr.
    And strangely open'd: what says now my monster,
    The multitude? they reel now, do they not?

Nun.
    Their gall is gone, and now they 'gin to weep
    The mischief they have done.

Arr. I thank 'em, rogues.

Nun.
    Part are so stupid, or so flexible,
    As they believe him innocent; all grieve:
    And some whose hands yet reek with his warm blood,
    And gripe the part which they did tear of him,
    Wish him collected and created new.

Lep.
    How Fortune plies her sports, when she begins
    To practise them! pursues, continues, adds,
    Confounds with varying her impassion'd moods!

Arr.
    Dost thou hope, Fortune, to redeem thy crimes,
    To make amend for thy ill-placed favours,
    With these strange punishments? Forbear, you things
    That stand upon the pinnacles of state,
    To boast your slippery height; when you do fall,
    You pash yourselves in pieces, ne'er to rise;
    And he that lends you pity, is not wise.

Ter.
    Let this example move the insolent man,
    Not to grow proud and careless of the gods.
    It is an odious wisdom to blaspheme,
    Much more to slighten, or deny their powers:

For, whom the morning saw so great and high,
Thus low and little, fore the even doth lie.   [Exeunt